The TESTIMONY *of the* EVANGELISTS

The
TESTIMONY
of the
EVANGELISTS

The Gospels Examined by the Rules of
Evidence Administered in Courts of Justice

by

Simon Greenleaf

and

A Review of the Trial of Jesus

in articles by

Simon Greenleaf
Joseph Salvador
M. Dupin

and

The Various Versions of the Bible

by

Constantine Tischendorff

kregel
CLASSICS

Grand Rapids, MI 49501

The Testimony of the Evangelists: The Gospels Examined by the Rules of Evidence Administered in Courts of Justice by Simon Greenleaf.

Copyright © 1995 and published by Kregel Classics, a division of Kregel, Inc., P.O. Box 2607, Grand Rapids, MI 49501.

Cover photo: COMSTOCK, INC.

Library of Congress Cataloging-in-Publication Data
[The testimony of the evangelists: the four Gospels examined by the rules of evidence].
Greenleaf, Simon, 1783–1853.
   The testimony of the evangelists: the gospels examined by the rules of evdence administered in courts of justice / Simon Greenleaf.
      p.   cm.
Originally published: New York: J. C. & Co., 1874.
   1. Bible. N.T. Gospels—Evidences, authority, etc. 2. Bible. N.T. Gospels—Harmonies, English. 3. Jesus Christ—Trial. 4. Apologetics—19th century. I. Title.
BS2560.G72   1995   226'.01—dc20   94-38149
                                                                                CIP
ISBN 978-0-8254-2747-3

7 8 9 10 / 13

Printed in the United States of America

Contents

Testimonials

The author is a lawyer, very learned in his profession, acute, critical, and used to raising and meeting practical doubts. Author of a treatise on the law of evidence, which has become a classic in the hands of the profession which he adorns, and teacher in one of the Law Seminaries which do honor to our country in the eyes of Europe, he brings rare qualifications for the task he assumes. Such are our views of this work which we commend to all; to the legal profession, from the character of its topics and the rank of its author to men desirous of knowledge, in every rank in life, because of its presenting this subject under such treatment as is applied to every day practical questions. It does not touch the intrinsic evidences of the Gospel: those which to the believer are, after all, the highest proofs. But it is to be remembered, that these are proofs which are not satisfactory until an examination of the outward evidence has led men to the conviction, that the Gospels cannot be false.

—Extract from the *New York Observer*

It is the production of an able and profound lawyer, a man who has grown gray in the halls of justice and the schools of jurisprudence; a writer of the highest authority on legal subjects, whose life has been spent in weighing testimony and sifting evidence, and whose published opinions on the rules of evidence are received as authoritative in all the English and American tribunals; for fourteen years the highly respected colleague of the late Mr. Justice Story, and also the honored head of the most distinguished and prosperous school of English law in the world.   —*North American Review*

It is no mean honor to America that her schools of jurisprudence have produced two of the first writers and best esteemed legal authorities of this century—the great and good man, Judge Story, and his worthy and eminent associate, Professor Greenleaf. Upon the existing *Law of Evidence* (by Greenleaf) more light has shone from the New World than from all the lawyers who adorn the courts of Europe.   —*London Law Magazine*

To the Members of the Legal Profession

Gentlemen,

The subject of the following work I hope will not be deemed so foreign to our professional pursuits, as to render it improper for me to dedicate it, as I now respectfully do, to you. If a close examination of the evidences of Christianity may be expected of one class of men more than another, it would seem incumbent on us, who make the law of evidence one of our peculiar studies. Our profession leads us to explore the mazes of falsehood, to detect its artifices, to pierce its thickest veils, to follow and expose its sophistries, to compare the statements of different witnesses with severity, to discover truth and separate it from error. Our fellow men are well aware of this; and probably they act upon this knowledge more generally, and with a more profound repose, than we are in the habit of considering. The influence, too, of the legal profession upon the community is unquestionably great; conversant, as it daily is, with all classes and grades of men, in their domestic and social relations, and in all the affairs of life, from the cradle to the grave. This influence we are constantly exerting for good or ill; and hence, to refuse to acquaint

ourselves with the evidences of the Christian religion, or to act as
though, having fully examined, we lightly esteemed them, is to assume an appalling amount of responsibility.

The things related by the Evangelists are certainly of the most
momentous character, affecting the principles of our conduct here,
and our happiness forever. The religion of Jesus Christ aims at nothing less than the utter overthrow of all other systems of religion in
the world; denouncing them as inadequate to the wants of man, false
in their foundations, and dangerous in their tendency. It not only
solicits the grave attention of all, to whom its doctrines are presented,
but it demands their cordial belief, as a matter of vital concernment.
These are no ordinary claims; and it seems hardly possible for a
rational being to regard them with even a subdued interest; much
less to treat them with mere indifference and contempt. If not true,
they are little else than the pretensions of a bold imposture, which,
not satisfied with having already enslaved millions of the human
race, seeks to continue its encroachments upon human liberty, until
all nations shall be subjugated under its iron rule. But if they are
well-founded and just, they can be no less than the high require-
ments of heaven, addressed by the voice of God to the reason and
understanding of man, concerning things deeply affecting his relations to his sovereign, and essential to the formation of his character
and of course to his destiny, both for this life and for the life to
come. Such was the estimate taken of religion, even the religion of
pagan Rome, by one of the greatest lawyers of antiquity, when he
argued that it was either nothing at all, or was everything. *Aut
undique religionem tolle, aut usquequaque conserva.*[1]

With this view of the importance of the subject, and in the hope
that the present work may in some degree aid or at least incite others
to a more successful pursuit of this interesting study, it is submitted
to your kind regard, by

Your obedient servant,
Simon Greenleaf

Notes
1. Cicero, Philip, II. § 43.

An Examination of the Testimony of the Evangelists

§ 1. In examining the evidences of the Christian religion, it is essential to the discovery of truth that we bring to the investigation a mind freed, as far as possible, from existing prejudice, and open to conviction. There should be a readiness, on our part, to investigate with candor, to follow the truth wherever it may lead us, and to submit, without reserve or objection, to all the teachings of this religion, if it be found to be of divine origin. "There is no other entrance," says Lord Bacon, "to the kingdom of man, which is founded in the sciences, than to the kingdom of heaven, into which no one can enter but in the character of a little child."[1] The docility which true philosophy requires of her disciples is not a spirit of servility, or the surrender of the reason and judgment to whatsoever the teacher may inculcate; but it is a mind free from all pride of opinion, not hostile to the truth sought for, willing to pursue the inquiry, and impartially to weigh the arguments and evidence, and to acquiesce in the judgment of right reason. The investigation, moreover, should be pursued with the serious earnestness which becomes the greatness of the subject—a subject fraught with such momentous consequences to man. It should be pursued as in the presence of God, and under the solemn sanctions created by a lively sense of his omniscience, and of our accountability to him for the right use of the faculties which he has bestowed.

§ 2. In requiring this candor and simplicity of mind in those who would investigate the truth of our religion, Christianity demands nothing more than is readily conceded to every branch of human science. All these have their data, and their axioms; and Christianity, too, has her first principles, the admission of which is essential to any real progress in knowledge. "Christianity," says Bishop Wilson, "inscribes on the portal of her dominion 'Whosoever shall not receive the kingdom of God as a little child, shall in nowise enter therein.' Christianity does not profess to convince the perverse and headstrong, to bring irresistible evidence to the daring and profane, to vanquish the proud scorner, and afford evidences from which the careless and perverse cannot possibly escape. This might go to destroy man's responsibility. All that Christianity professes, is to propose such evidences as may satisfy the meek, the tractable, the candid, the serious inquirer."[2]

§ 3. The present design, however, is not to enter upon any general examination of the evidences of Christianity, but to confine the inquiry to the testimony of the Four Evangelists, bringing their narratives to the tests to which other evidence is subjected in human tribunals. The foundation of our religion is a basis of fact—the fact, of the birth, ministry, miracles, death, resurrection, and ascension of Jesus Christ. These are related by the Evangelists as having actually occurred, within their own personal knowledge. Our religion, then, rests on the credit due to these witnesses. Are they worthy of implicit belief, in the matters which they relate? This is the question, in all human tribunals, in regard to persons testifying before them; and we propose to test the veracity of these witnesses, by the same rules and means which are there employed. The importance of the facts testified, and their relations to the affairs of the soul, and the life to come, can make no difference in the principles or the mode of weighing the evidence. It is still the evidence of matters of fact, capable of being seen and known and related, as well by one man as by another. And if the testimony of the Evangelist, supposing it to be relevant and material to the issue in a question of property or of personal right, between man and man, in a court of justice, ought to be believed and have weight; then, upon the like principles, it ought to receive our entire credit here. But, if, on the other hand, we should be justified in rejecting it, if there testified on oath, then, supposing our rules of evidence to be sound, we may be excused if we hesitate elsewhere to give it credence.

§ 4. The proof that God has revealed himself to man by special and express communications, and that Christianity constitutes that revelation, is no part of these inquiries. This has already been shown, in the most satisfactory manner, by others, who have written expressly upon this subject.[3] Referring therefore to their writings for the arguments and proofs, the fact will here be assumed as true. That man is a religious being, is universally conceded, for it has been seen to be universally true. He is everywhere a worshiper. In every age and country, and in every stage, from the highest intellectual culture to the darkest stupidity, he bows with homage to a superior Being. Be it the rude-carved idol of his own fabrication, or, the unseen divinity that stirs within him, it is still the object of his adoration. This trait in the character of man is so uniform, that it may safely be assumed, either as one of the original attributes of his nature, or as necessarily resulting from the action of one or more of those attributes.

§ 5. The object of man's worship, whatever it be, will naturally be his standard of perfection. He clothes it with every attribute, belonging, in his view, to a perfect character; and this character he himself endeavors to attain. He may not, directly and consciously, aim to acquire every virtue of his deity, and to avoid the opposite vices; but still this will be the inevitable consequence of sincere and constant worship. As in human society men become assimilated, both in manners and in moral principles, to their chosen associates, so in the worship of whatever deity men adore, they "form to him the relish of their souls." To suppose, then, that God made man capable of religion, and requiring it in order to the development of the highest part of his nature, without communicating with him, as a father, in those revelations which alone could perfect that nature, would be a reproach upon God, and a contradiction.[4]

§ 6. How it came to pass that man, originally taught, as we doubt not he was, to know and to worship the true Jehovah, is found, at so early a period of his history, a worshiper of baser objects, it is foreign to our present purpose to inquire. But the fact is lamentably true, that he soon became an idolator, a worshiper of moral abominations. The Scythians and Northmen adored the impersonations of heroic valor and of bloodthirsty and cruel revenge. The mythology of Greece and of Rome, though it exhibited a few examples of virtue and goodness, abounded in others of gross licentiousness and vice. The gods of Egypt were reptiles and beasts and birds. The religion of Central and Eastern Asia was polluted with lust and cruelty, and smeared with blood, rioting in deadly triumph, over all the tender affections of the human heart and all the convictions of the human understanding. Western and Southern Africa and Polynesia are, to this day, the abodes of frightful idolatry, cannibalism, and cruelty; and the aborigines of both the Americas are examples of the depths of superstition to which the human mind may be debased. In every quarter of the world, however, there is a striking uniformity seen in all the features of paganism. The ruling principle of its religion is terror, and its deity is lewd and cruel. Whatever of purity the earlier forms of paganism may have possessed, it is evident from history that it was of brief duration. Every form, which history has preserved, grew rapidly and steadily worse and more corrupt, until the entire heathen world, before the coming of Christ, was infected with that loathsome leprosy of pollution, described with revolting vividness by St. Paul, in the beginning of his Epistle to the Romans.

§ 7. So general and decided was this proclivity to the worship of strange gods, that, at the time of the deluge, only one family remained faithful to Jehovah; and this was a family which had been favored with his special revelation. Indeed it is evident that nothing but a revelation from God could raise men from the degradation of pagan idolatry, because nothing else has ever had that effect. If man could achieve his own freedom from this bondage, he would long since have been free.

But instead of this, the increase of light and civilization and refinement in the pagan world has but multiplied the objects of his worship, added voluptuous refinements to its ritual, and thus increased the number and weight of his chains. In this respect there is no difference in their moral condition, between the barbarous Scythian and the learned Egyptian or Roman of ancient times, nor between the ignorant African and the polished Hindu of our own day. The only method, which has been successfully employed to deliver man from idolatry, is that of presenting to the eye of his soul an object of worship perfectly holy and pure, directly opposite, in moral character, to the gods he had formerly adored. He could not transfer to his deities a better character than be himself possessed. He must forever remain enslaved to his idols, unless a new and pure object of worship were revealed to him, with a display of superior power sufficient to overcome his former faith and present fears, to detach his affections from grosser objects, and to fix them upon that which alone is worthy.[5] This is precisely what God, as stated in the Holy Scriptures, has done. He rescued one family from idolatry in the Old World, by the revelation of himself to Noah; he called a distinct branch of this family to the knowledge of himself, in the person of Abraham and his sons; he extended this favor to a whole nation, through the ministry of Moses; but it was through that of Jesus Christ alone that it was communicated to the whole world. In Egypt, by the destruction of all the objects of the popular worship, God taught the Israelites that he alone was the self-existent Almighty. At the Red Sea, he emphatically showed them that he was the Protector and Savior of his people. At Sinai, he revealed himself as the righteous Governor, who required implicit obedience for men, and taught them, by the strongly-marked distinctions of the ceremonial law, that he was a holy Being, of purer eyes than to behold evil, and that could not look upon iniquity. The demerit of sin was inculcated by the solemn infliction of death upon every animal, offered as a propitiatory sacrifice. And when, by this system of instruction, he had prepared a people to receive the perfect revelation of the character of God, of the nature of his worship, and of the way of restoration to his image and favor, this also was expressly revealed by the mission of his Son.[6]

§ 8. That the books of the Old Testament, as we now have them, are genuine; that they existed in the time of our Savior, and were commonly received and referred to among the Jews as the sacred books of their religion,[7] and that the text of the Four Evangelists has been handed down to us in the state in which it was originally written that is, without having been materially corrupted or falsified, either by heretics or Christians; are facts which we are entitled to assume as true, until the contrary is shown.

The genuineness of these writings really admits of as little doubt, and is susceptible of as ready proof, as that of any ancient writings whatever. The rule of municipal law on this subject is familiar, and applies with equal force to all ancient writings, whether documentary or otherwise; and as it comes first in order, in the prosecution of these inquiries, it may, for the sake of mere convenience, be designated as our first rule:

Every document, apparently ancient, coming from the proper repository or custody, and bearing on its face no evident marks of forgery, the law presumes to be genuine, and devolves on the opposing party the burden of proving it to be otherwise.

§ 9. An ancient document, offered in evidence in our courts, is said to come from the proper repository, when it is found in the place where, and under the care of persons with whom, such writings might naturally and reasonably be expected to be found; for it is this custody which gives authenticity to documents found within it.[8] If they come from such a place, and bear no evident marks of forgery, the law presumes that they are genuine, and they are permitted to be read in evidence, unless the opposing party is able successfully to impeach them.[9] The burden of showing them to be false and unworthy of credit, is devolved on the party who makes that objection. The presumption of law is the judgment of charity. It presumes that every man is innocent until he is proved guilty; that everything has been done fairly and legally, until it is proved to have been otherwise; and that every document, found in its proper repository, and not bearing marks of forgery, is genuine. Now this is precisely the case with the Sacred Writings. They have been used in the church from time immemorial, and thus are found in the place where alone they ought to be looked for. They come to us, and challenge our reception of them as genuine writings, precisely as *Domesday Book,* the *Ancient Statutes of Wales,* or any other of the ancient documents which have recently been published under the British Record Commission, are received. They are found in familiar use in all the churches of Christendom, as the sacred books to which all denominations of Christians refer, as the standard of their faith. There is no pretense that they were engraven on plates of gold and discovered in a cave, nor that they were brought from heaven by angels; but they are received as the plain narratives and writings of the men whose names they respectively bear, made public at the time they were written and though there are some slight discrepancies among the copies subsequently made, there is no pretense that the originals were anywhere corrupted. If it be objected that the originals are lost, and that copies alone are now produced, the principles of the municipal law here also afford a satisfactory answer. For the multiplication of copies was a public fact, in the faithfulness of which all the Christian community had an interest; and it is a rule of law, that:

In matters of public and general interest, all persons must be presumed to be conversant, on the principle that individuals are presumed to be conversant with their own affairs.

Therefore it is that, in such matters, the prevailing current of assertion is resorted to as evidence, for it is to this that every member of the community is supposed to be privy.[10] The persons, moreover, who multiplied these copies, may be regarded, in some manner, as the agents of the Christian public, for whose use and benefit the copies were made; and on the ground of the credit due to such agents, and of the public nature of the facts themselves, the copies thus made are entitled to an extraordinary degree of confidence, and, as in the case of official registers and other public books, it is not necessary that they should be confirmed and sanctioned by the ordinary tests of truth.[11] If any ancient document concerning our public rights were lost, copies which had been as universally received and acted upon as the Four Gospels have been, would have been received in evidence in any of our courts of justice, without the slightest hesitation. The entire text of the *Corpus Juris Civilis* is received as authority in all the courts of continental Europe, upon much weaker evidence of its genuineness; for the integrity of the Sacred Text has been preserved by the jealousy of opposing sects, beyond any moral possibility of corruption; while that of the Roman Civil Law has been preserved by tacit consent without the interest of any opposing school, to watch over and preserve it from alteration.

§ 10 These copies of the Holy Scriptures having thus been in familiar use in the churches, from the time when the text was committed to writing; having been watched with vigilance by so many sects, opposed to each other in doctrine, yet all appealing to these Scriptures for the correctness of their faith; and having in all ages, down to this day, been respected as the authoritative source of all ecclesiastical power and government, and submitted to, and acted under in regard to so many claims of right, on the one hand, and so many obligations of duty, on the other; it is quite erroneous to suppose that the Christian is bound to offer any further proof of their genuineness or authenticity. It is for the objector to show them spurious; for on him, by the plainest rules of law, lies the burden of proof.[12] If it were the case of a claim to a franchise, and a copy of an ancient deed or charter were produced in support of the title, under parallel circumstances on which to presume its genuineness, no lawyer, it is believed, would venture to deny either its admissibility in evidence, or the satisfactory character of the proof. In a recent case in the House of Lords, precisely such a document, being an old manuscript copy, purporting to have been extracted from ancient Journals of the House, which were lost, and to have been made by an officer whose duty it was to prepare lists of the Peers, was held admissible in a claim of peerage.[13]

§ 11. Supposing, therefore, that it is not irrational, nor inconsistent with sound philosophy, to believe that God has made a special and express revelation of his character and will to man, and that the sacred books of our religion are genuine, as we now have them we proceed to examine and compare the testimony of Four Evangelists, as witnesses to the life and doctrines of Jesus Christ; in order to determine the degree of credit, to which, by the rules of evidence applied in human tribunals, they are justly entitled. Our attention will naturally be first directed to the witnesses themselves, to see who and what manner of men they were; and we shall take them in the order of their writings; stating the prominent traits only in their lives and characters, as they are handed down to us by credible historians.

§ 12. Matthew, called also Levi, was a Jew of Galilee, but of what city is uncertain. He held the place of publican, or tax-gatherer, under the Roman government, and his office seems to have consisted in collecting the taxes within his district, as well as the duties and customs levied on goods and persons, passing in and out of his district or province, across the lake of Genesareth. While engaged in this business, at the office or usual place of collection, he was required by Jesus to follow him, as one of his disciples; a command which he immediately obeyed. Soon afterwards, he appears to have given a great entertainment to his fellow-publicans and friends, at which Jesus was present; intending probably both to celebrate his own change of profession, and to give them an opportunity to profit by the teaching of his new Master.[14] He was constituted one of the twelve apostles, and constantly attended the person of Jesus as a faithful follower, until the crucifixion; and after the ascension of his Master he preached the gospel for some time with other apostles, in Judea, and afterwards in Ethiopia, where he died.

He is generally allowed to have written first of all the evangelists; but whether in the Hebrew or the Greek language, or in both, the learned are not agreed nor is it material to our purpose to inquire; the genuineness of our present Greek gospel being sustained by satisfactory evidence.[15] The precise time when he wrote is also uncertain, the several dates given to it among learned men, varying from A.D. 37 to A.D. 64. The earlier date, however, is argued with greater force, from the improbability that the Christians would be left for several years without a general and authentic history of our Savior's ministry; from the evident allusions which it contains to a state of persecution in the church at the time it was written; from the titles of sanctity ascribed to Jerusalem, and a higher veneration testified for the temple than is found in the other and later evangelists from the comparative gentleness with which Herod's character and conduct are dealt with, that bad prince probably being still in power and from the frequent mention of Pilate, as still governor of Judea.[16]

§ 13. That Matthew was himself a native Jew, familiar with the opinions, ceremonies, and customs of his countrymen; that he was conversant with the Sacred Writings, and habituated to their idiom; a man of plain sense, but of little learning, except what he derived from the Scriptures of the Old Testament; that he wrote seriously and from conviction, and had, on most occasions, been present, and attended closely, to the transactions which he relates, and relates, too, without any view of applause to himself; are facts which we may consider established by internal evidence, as strong as the nature of the case will admit. It is deemed equally well proved, both by internal evidence and the aid of history, that he wrote for the use of his countrymen the Jews. Every circumstance is noticed which might conciliate their belief, and every unnecessary expression is avoided which might obstruct it. They looked for the Messiah, of the lineage of David, and born in Bethlehem, in the circumstances of whose life the prophecies should find fulfillment, a matter, in their estimation, of peculiar value: and to all these this evangelist has directed their especial attention.[17]

§ 14. Allusion has been already made to his employment as a collector of taxes and customs but the subject is too important to be passed over without further notice. The tribute imposed by the Romans upon countries conquered by their arms was enormous. In the time of Pompey, the sums annually exacted from their Asiatic provinces, of which Judea was one, amounted to about four millions and a half of sterling, or about twenty-two millions of dollars. These exactions were made in the usual forms of direct and indirect taxation; the rate of the customs on merchandise varying from, an eighth to a fortieth part of the value of the commodity; and the tariff including all the principal articles of the commerce of the East, much of which, as is well known, still found its way to Italy through Palestine, as well as by the way of Damascus and of Egypt. The direct taxes consisted of a capitation-tax, and a land-tax, assessed upon a valuation or census, periodically taken, under the oath of the individual, with heavy penal sanctions.[18] It is natural to suppose that these taxes were not voluntarily paid, especially since they were imposed by the conqueror upon a conquered people, and by a heathen, too, upon the people of the house of Israel. The increase of taxes has generally been found to multiply discontents, evasions, and frauds on the one hand, and, on the other, to increase vigilance, suspicion, close scrutiny, and severity of exaction. The penal code, as revised by Theodosius, will give us some notion of the difficulties in the way of the revenue officers, in the earlier times of which we are speaking. These difficulties must have been increased by the fact that, at this period, a considerable portion of the commerce of that part of the world was carried on by the Greeks, whose ingenuity and want of faith were proverbial. It was to such an employment and under such circumstances, that Matthew was educated; an employment which must have made him acquainted with the Greek language, and extensively conversant with the public affairs and the men of business of his time; thus entitling him to our confidence, as an experienced and intelligent observer of events passing before him. And if the men of that day were, as in truth they appear to have been, as much disposed as those of the present time, to evade the payment of public taxes and duties, and to elude, by all possible means, the vigilance of the revenue officers, Matthew must have been familiar with a great variety of forms of fraud, imposture, cunning, and deception, and must have become habitually distrustful, scrutinizing, and cautious; and, of course, much less likely to have been deceived in regard to many of the facts in our Lord's ministry, extraordinary as they were, which fell under his observation. This circumstance shows both the sincerity and the wisdom of Jesus in selecting him for an eye-witness of his conduct, and adds great weight to the value of the testimony of this evangelist.

§ 15. Mark was the son of a pious sister of Barnabas, named Mary, who dwelt at Jerusalem, and at whose house the early Christians often assembled. His Hebrew name was John; the surname of Mark having been adopted, as is supposed, when he left Judea to preach the gospel in foreign countries; a practice not unusual among the Jews of that age, who frequently, upon such occasions, assumed a name more familiar than their own to the people whom they visited. He is supposed to have been converted to the Christian faith by the ministry of Peter. He traveled from Jerusalem to Antioch with Paul and Barnabas, and afterwards accompanied them elsewhere. When they landed at Perga in Pamphylia, he left them and returned to Jerusalem; for which reason, when he afterwards would have gone with them, Paul refused to take him. Upon this, a difference of opinion arose between the two apostles, and they separated, Barnabas taking Mark with him to Cyprus. Subsequently he accompanied Timothy to Rome, at the express desire of Paul. From this city he probably went into Asia, where he found Peter, with whom he returned to Rome, in which city he is supposed to have written and published his Gospel. Such is the outline of his history, as it is furnished by the New Testament.[19] The early historians add, that after this he went into Egypt and planted a church in Alexandria, where he died.[20]

§ 16. It is agreed that Mark wrote his Gospel for the use of Gentile converts; an opinion deriving great force from the explanations introduced into it, which would have been useless to a Jew;[21] and that it was composed for those at Rome is believed, not only from the numerous Latinisms it contains, but from the unanimous testimony of ancient writers, and from the internal evidence afforded by the Gospel itself.

§ 17. Some have entertained the opinion that Mark compiled his account from that of Matthew, of which they supposed it an abridgment. But this notion has been refuted by Koppe, and others,[22] and is now generally regarded as untenable. For Mark frequently deviates from Matthew in the order of time; in his arrangement of facts; and he adds many things not related by the other evangelists; neither of which a mere epitomizer would probably have done. He also omits several things related by Matthew, and imperfectly describes others, especially the transactions of Christ with the apostles after the resurrection; giving no account whatever of his appearance in Galilee; omissions irreconcilable with any previous knowledge of the Gospel according to Matthew. To these proofs we may add, that in several places there are discrepancies between the accounts of Matthew and Mark, not, indeed, irreconcilable, but sufficient to destroy the probability that the latter copied from the former.[23] The striking coincidences between them, in style, words, and things, in other places, may be accounted for by considering that Peter, who is supposed to have dictated this Gospel to Mark, was quite as intimately acquainted as Matthew with the miracles and discourses of our Lord; which, therefore he would naturally recite in his preaching; and that the same things might very naturally be related in the same manner, by men who sought not after excellency of speech. Peter's agency in the narrative of Mark is asserted by all ancient writers, and is confirmed by the fact that his humility is conspicuous in every part of it, where anything is or might be related of him; his weaknesses and fall being fully exposed, while things which might redound to his honor, are either omitted or but slightly mentioned; that scarcely any transaction of Jesus is related, at which Peter was not present, and that all are related with that circumstantial minuteness which belongs to the testimony of an eye-witness.[24] We may, therefore, regard the Gospel of Mark as an original composition, written at the dictation of Peter, and consequently as another original narrative of the life, miracles, and doctrines of our Lord.

§ 18. Luke, according to Eusebius, was a native of Antioch, by profession a physician, and for a considerable period a companion of the apostle Paul. From the casual notices of him in the Scriptures, and from the early Christian writers, it has been collected, that his parents were Gentiles, but that he in his youth embraced Judaism, from which he was converted to Christianity. The first mention of him is that he was with Paul at Troas;[25] whence he appears to have attended him to Jerusalem; continued with him in all his troubles in Judea; and sailed with him where he was sent a prisoner from Caesarea to Rome, where he remained with him during his two years' confinement. As none of the ancient fathers have mentioned his having suffered martyrdom, it is generally supposed that he died a natural death.

§ 19. That he wrote his Gospel for the benefit of Gentile converts is affirmed by the unanimous voice of Christian antiquity; and it may also be inferred from its dedication to a Gentile. He is particularly careful to specify various circumstances conducive to the information of strangers, but not so to the Jews; he gives the lineage of Jesus upward, after the manner of the Gentiles instead of downward, as Matthew had done; tracing it up to Adam, and thus showing that Jesus was the promised seed of the woman; and he marks the eras of his birth, and of the ministry of John by the reigns of the Roman emperors. He also has introduced several things, not mentioned by the other evangelists, but highly encouraging to the Gentiles to turn to God in the hope of pardon and acceptance; of which description are the parables of the publican and Pharisee, in the temple; the lost piece of silver; and the prodigal son; and the fact of Christ's visit to Zaccheus the publican, and the pardon of the penitent thief.

§ 20. That Luke was a physician appears not only from the testimony of Paul,[26] but from the internal marks in his Gospel, showing that he was both an acute observer, and had given particular and even professional attention to all our Savior's miracles of healing. Thus, the man whom Matthew and Mark describe simply as a leper, Luke describes as *full* of leprosy;[27] he, whom they mention as having a withered hand, Luke says had his *right* hand withered;[28] and of the maid, of whom the others say that Jesus took her by the hand and she arose, he adds, that *her spirit came to her again.*[29] He alone, with professional accuracy of observation, says that *virtue went out* of Jesus, and healed the sick;[30] he alone states the fact that the sleep of the disciples in Gethsemane was *induced by extreme sorrow;* and mentions the blood-like sweat of Jesus, as occasioned by the *intensity of his agony;* and he alone relates the miraculous healing of Malchus's ear.[31] That he was also a man of a liberal education, the comparative elegance of his writings sufficiently shows.[32]

§ 21. The design of Luke's Gospel was to supersede the defective and inaccurate narratives then in circulation, and to deliver to Theophilus to whom it is addressed, a full and authentic account of the life, doctrines, miracles, death, and resurrection of our Savior. Who Theophilus was, the learned are not perfectly agreed; but the most probable opinion is that of Dr. Lardner, now generally adopted, that, as Luke wrote his Gospel in Greece, Theophilus was a man of rank in that country.[33] Either the relations subsisting between him and Luke, or the dignity and power of his rank, or both, induced the evangelist, who himself also "had perfect understanding of all things from the first," to devote the utmost care to the drawing up of a complete and authentic narrative of these great events. He does not affirm himself to have been an eye-witness; though his personal knowledge of some of the transactions may well be inferred from the "perfect understanding" which he says he possessed. Some of the learned seem to have drawn this inference as to them all, and to have placed him in the class of original witnesses but this opinion though maintained on strong and plausible grounds, is not generally adopted. If, then, he did not write from his own personal knowledge the question is, what is the legal character of his testimony?

§ 22. If it were "the result of inquiries, made under competent public authority, concerning matters in which the public are concerned,"[34] it would possess every legal attribute of an inquisition, and, as such, would be legally admissible in evidence, in a court of justice. To entitle such results, however, to our full confidence, it is not necessary that they should be obtained under a legal commission; it is sufficient if the inquiry is gravely undertaken and pursued, by a person of competent intelligence, sagacity, and integrity. The request of a person in authority, or a desire to serve the public, are, to all moral intents, as sufficient a motive as a legal commission.[35] Thus, we know that when complaint is made to the head of a department, of official misconduct or abuse, existing in some remote quarter, nothing is more common than to send some confidential person to the spot, to ascertain the facts and report them to the department; and this report is confidently adopted as the basis of its discretionary action, in the correction of the abuse, or the removal of the offender. Indeed, the result of any grave inquiry is equally certain to receive our confidence, though it may have been voluntarily undertaken, if the party making it had access to the means of complete and satisfactory information upon the subject.[36] If, therefore, Luke's Gospel were to be regarded only as the work of a contemporary historian, it would be entitled to our confidence. But it is more than this. It is the result of careful inquiry and examination, made by a person of science, intelligence, and education, concerning subjects which he was perfectly competent to investigate, and as to many of which he was peculiarly skilled, they being cases of the cure of maladies; subjects, too, of which he already had the perfect knowledge of a contemporary, and perhaps an eye-witness, but beyond doubt, familiar with the parties concerned in the transactions, and belonging to the community in which the events transpired, which were in the mouths of all; and the narrative, moreover, drawn up for the especial use, and probably at the request, of a man of distinction, whom it would not be for the interest nor safety of the writer to deceive or mislead. Such a document certainly possesses all the moral attributes of an inquest of office, or of any other official investigation of facts; and as such is entitled, *in foro conscientiae*, to be adduced as original, competent, and satisfactory evidence of the matters it contains.

§ 23. John, the last of the evangelists, was the son of Zebedee, a fisherman of the town of Bethsaida, on the sea of Galilee. His father appears to have been a respectable man in his calling, owning his vessel and having hired servants.[37] His mother, too, was among those who followed Jesus, and "ministered unto him;"[38] and to John himself, Jesus, when on the cross, confided the care and support of his own mother.[39] This disciple also seems to have been favorably known to the high priest, and to have influence in his family; by means of which he had the privilege of being present in his palace at the examination of his Master, and of introducing also Peter, his friend.[40] He was the youngest of the apostles; was eminently the object of the Lord's regard and confidence; was on various occasions admitted to free and intimate communion with him; and is described as "the disciple whom Jesus loved."[41] Hence he was present at several scenes, to which most of the others were not admitted. He alone, in company with Peter and James, was present at the resurrection of Jairus's daughter, at the transfiguration on the mount, and at the agony of our Savior in the garden of Gethsemane.[42] He was the only apostle who followed Jesus to the cross, he was the first of them at the sepulcher, and he was present at the several appearances of our Lord after his resurrection. These circumstances, together with his intimate friendship with the mother of Jesus, especially qualify him to give a circumstantial and authentic account of the life of his Master. After the ascension of Christ, and the effusion of the Holy Spirit on the day of Pentecost, John became one of the chief apostles of the circumcision, exercising his ministry in and near Jerusalem. From ecclesiastical history we learn that after the death of Mary the mother of Jesus, he proceeded to Asia Minor, where he founded and presided over seven churches, in as many cities, but resided chiefly at Ephesus. Thence he was banished, in Domitian's reign, to the isle of Patmos, where he wrote his Revelation. On the accession of Nerva he was freed from exile, and returned to Ephesus, where he wrote his Gospel and Epistles, and died at the age of one hundred years, about A.D. 100; in the third year of the emperor Trajan.[43]

§ 24. The learned are not agreed as to the time when the Gospel of John was written; some dating it as early as the year 68, others as late as the year 98; but it is generally conceded to have been written after all the others. That it could not have been the work of some Platonic Christian of a subsequent age, as some have without evidence asserted, is manifest from references to it by some of the early fathers, and from the concurring testimony of many other writers of the ancient Christian church.[44]

§ 25. That it was written either with especial reference to the Gentiles, or at a period when very many of them had become converts to Christianity, is inferred from the various explanations it contains, beyond the other Gospels, which could have been necessary only to persons unacquainted with Jewish names and customs.[45] And that it was written after all the others, and to supply their omissions, is concluded, not only from the uniform tradition and belief in the church, but from his studied omission of most of the transactions noticed by the others, and from his care to mention several incidents which they have not recorded. That their narratives were known to him, is too evident to admit of doubt; while his omission to repeat what they had already stated, or, where he does mention the same things, his relating them in a brief and cursory manner, affords incidental but strong testimony that he regarded their accounts as faithful and true.[46]

§ 26. Such are the brief histories of men, whose narratives we are to examine and compare; conducting the examination and weighing the testimony by the same rules and principles which govern our tribunals of justice in similar cases. These tribunals are in such cases governed by the following fundamental rule:

In trials of fact, by oral testimony, the proper inquiry is not whether it is possible that the testimony may be false, but whether there is sufficient probability that it is true.

It should be observed that the subject of inquiry is a matter of fact, and not of abstract mathematical truth. The latter alone is susceptible of that high degree of proof, usually termed demonstration, which excludes the possibility of error, and which therefore may reasonably be required in support of every mathematical deduction. But the proof of matters of fact rests upon moral evidence alone; by which is meant not merely that species of evidence which we do not obtain either from our own senses, from intuition, or from demonstration. In the ordinary affairs of life we do not require nor expect demonstrative evidence, because it is inconsistent with the nature of matters of fact, and to insist on its production would be unreasonable and absurd. And it makes no difference, whether the facts to be proved relate to this life or to the next, the nature of the evidence required being in both cases the same. The error of the skeptic consists in pretending or supposing that there is a difference in the nature of the things to be proved; and in demanding demonstrative evidence concerning things which are not susceptible of any other than moral evidence alone, and of which the utmost that can be said is, that there is no reasonable doubt about their truth.[47]

§ 27. In proceeding to weigh the evidence of any proposition of fact, the previous question to be determined is, when may it be said to be proved? The answer to this question is furnished by another rule of municipal law, which may be thus stated:

A proposition of fact is proved, when its truth is established by competent and satisfactory evidence.

By competent evidence is meant such as the nature of the thing to be proved requires; and by satisfactory evidence is meant that amount of proof, which ordinarily satisfies an unprejudiced mind, beyond any reasonable doubt. The circumstances which will amount to this degree of proof can never be previously defined; the only legal test to which they can be subjected is their sufficiency to satisfy the mind and conscience of a man of common prudence and discretion, and so to convince him, that he could venture to act upon that conviction in matters of the highest concern and importance to his own interest.[48] If, therefore, the subject is a problem in mathematics, its truth is to be shown by the certainty of demonstrative evidence. But if it is a question of fact in human affairs, nothing more than moral evidence can be required, for this is the best evidence which, from the nature of the case, is attainable. Now as the facts, stated in Scripture history, are not of the former kind, but are cognizable by the senses, they may be said to be proved when they are established by that kind and degree of evidence which, as we have just observed, would, in the affairs of human life, satisfy the mind and conscience of a common man. When we have this degree of evidence, it is unreasonable to require more. A juror would violate his oath, if he should refuse to acquit or condemn a person charged with an offense, where this measure of proof was adduced.

§ 28. Proceeding further, to inquire whether the facts related by the Four Evangelists are proved by competent and satisfactory evidence, we are led, first, to consider on which side lies the burden of establishing the credibility of the witnesses. On this point the municipal law furnishes a rule, which is of constant application in all trials by jury, and is indeed the dictate of that charity which thinketh no evil:

In the absence of circumstances which generate suspicion, every witness is to be presumed credible, until the contrary is shown; the burden of impeaching his credibility lying on the objector.[49]

This rule serves to show the injustice with which the writers of the Gospels have ever been treated by infidels; an injustice silently acquiesced in even by Christians; in requiring the Christian affirmatively, and by positive evidence, *aliunde*, to establish, the credibility of his witnesses above all others, before their testimony is entitled to be considered, and in permitting the testimony of a single profane writer, alone and uncorroborated, to outweigh that of any single Christian. This is not the course in courts of chancery, where the testimony of a single witness is never permitted to outweigh the oath even of the defendant himself, interested as he is in the cause but, on the contrary, if the plaintiff, after having required the oath of his adversary, cannot overthrow it by something more than the oath of one witness, however credible, it must stand as evidence against him. But the Christian writer seems, by the usual course of the argument, to have been deprived of the common presumption of charity in his favor; and reversing the ordinary rule of administering justice in human tribunals, his testimony is unjustly presumed to be false, until it is proved to be true. This treatment, moreover, has been applied to them all in a body; and, without due regard to the fact, that, being independent historians, writing at different periods, they are entitled to the support of each other: they have been treated, in the argument, almost as if the New Testament were the entire production, at once, of a body of men, conspiring by a joint fabrication, to impose a false religion upon the world. It is time that this injustice should cease; that the testimony of the evangelists should be admitted to be true, until it can be disproved by those who would impugn it; that the silence of one sacred writer on any point should no more detract from his own veracity or that of the other historians, than the like circumstance is permitted to do among profane writers; and that the Four Evangelists should be admitted in corroboration of each other, as readily as Josephus and Tacitus, or Polybius and Livy.[50]

§ 29. But if the burden of establishing the credibility of the evangelists were devolved on those who affirm the truth of their narratives, it is still capable of a ready moral demonstration, when we consider the nature and character of the testimony, and the essential marks of difference between true narratives of facts and the creations of falsehoods. It is universally admitted that the credit to be given to witnesses depends chiefly on their ability to discern and comprehend what was before them, their opportunities for observation, the degree of accuracy with which they are accustomed to mark passing events and their integrity in relating them. The rule of municipal law on this subject embraces all these particulars, and is thus stated by a legal text-writer of the highest repute:

> *The credit due to the testimony of witnesses depends upon, firstly, their honesty; secondly, their ability; thirdly, their number and the consistency of their testimony; fourthly, the conformity of their testimony with experience; and fifthly, the coincidence of their testimony with collateral circumstances.*[51]

Let the evangelists be tried by these tests.

§ 30. And *first*, as to their *honesty*. Here they are entitled to the benefit of the general course of human experience, that men ordinarily speak the truth, when they have no prevailing motive or inducement to the contrary. This presumption, to which we have before alluded, is applied in courts of justice, even to witnesses whose integrity is not wholly free from suspicion; much more is it applicable to the evangelists, whose testimony went against all their worldly interests. The great truths which the apostles declared were that Christ had risen from the dead, and that only through repentance from sin, and faith in him, could men hope for salvation. This doctrine they asserted with one voice, everywhere, not only under the greatest discouragements, but in the face of the most appalling terrors that can be presented to the mind of man. Their master had recently perished as a malefactor, by the sentence of a public tribunal. His religion sought to overthrow the religions of the whole world. The laws of every country were against the teachings of his disciples. The interests and passions of all the rulers and great men in the world were against them. The fashion of the world was against them. Propagating this new faith, even in the most inoffensive and peaceful manner, they could expect nothing but contempt, opposition, revilings, bitter persecutions, stripes, imprisonments, torments, and cruel deaths. Yet this faith they zealously did propagate; and all these miseries they endured undismayed, nay, rejoicing. As one after another was put to a miserable death, the survivors only prosecuted their work with increased vigor and resolution. The annals of military warfare afford scarcely an example of the like heroic constancy, patience, and unblenching courage. They had every possible motive to review carefully the grounds of their faith, and the evidences of the great facts and truths which they asserted and these motives were pressed upon their attention with the most melancholy and terrific frequency. It was therefore impossible that they could have persisted in affirming the truths they have narrated, had not Jesus actually risen from the dead, and had they not known this fact as certainly as they knew any other fact.[52] If it were morally possible for them to have been deceived in this matter, every human motive operated to lead them to discover and avow their error. To have persisted in so gross a falsehood, after it was known to them, was not only to encounter, for life, all the evils which man could inflict from without, but to endure also the pangs of inward and conscious guilt; with no hope of future peace, no testimony of a good conscience, no expectation of honor or esteem among men, no hope of happiness in this life, or in the world to come.

§ 31. Such conduct in the apostles would moreover have been utterly irreconcilable with the fact that they possessed the ordinary constitution of our common nature. Yet their lives do show them to have been men like all others of our race; swayed by the same motives, animated by the same hopes, affected by the same joys, subdued by the same sorrows, agitated by the same fears, and subject to the same passions, temptations, and infirmities as ourselves. And their writings show them to have been men of vigorous understandings. If then their testimony was not true, there was no possible motive for this fabrication.

§ 32. It would also have been irreconcilable with the fact that they were good men. But it is impossible to read their writings and not feel that we are conversing with men eminently holy and of tender consciences, with men acting under an abiding sense of the presence and omniscience of God, and of their accountability to him, living in his fear, and walking in his ways. Now, though in a single instance a good man may fall when under strong temptations, yet he is not found persisting, for years, in deliberate falsehood, asserted with the most solemn appeals to God, without the slightest temptation or motive, and against all the opposing interests which reign in the human breast. If, on the contrary, they are supposed to have been bad men, it is incredible that such men should have chosen this form of imposture, enjoining as it does unfeigned repentance, the utter forsaking and abhorrence of all falsehood and of every other sin, the practice of daily self-denial, self-abasement and self-sacrifice, the crucifixion of the flesh with all its earthly appetites and desires, indifference to the honors, and hearty contempt of the vanities of the world, and inculcating perfect purity of heart and life, and communion of the soul with heaven. It is incredible that bad men should invent falsehoods to promote the religion of the God of truth. The supposition is suicidal. If they did believe in a future state of retribution, a heaven and a hell hereafter, they took the most certain course, if false witnesses, to secure the latter for their portion. And if, still being bad men, they did not believe in future punishment, how came they to invent falsehoods the direct and certain tendency of which was to destroy all their prospects of worldly honor and happiness, and to insure their misery in this life? From these absurdities there is no escape, but in the perfect conviction and admission that they were good men, testifying to that which they had carefully observed and considered, and well knew to be true.[53]

§ 33. In the *second* place, as to their *ability*. The text writer before cited observes that the ability of a witness to speak the truth depends on the opportunities which he has had for observing the facts, the accuracy of his powers of discerning, and the faithfulness of his memory in retaining the facts, once observed and known.[54] Of the latter trait, in these witnesses we of course know nothing, nor have we any traditionary information in regard to the accuracy of their powers of discerning. But we may well suppose that in these respects they were like the generality of their countrymen, until the contrary is shown by an objector. It is always to be presumed that men are honest, and of sound mind, and of the average and ordinary degree of intelligence. This is not the judgment of mere charity; it is also the uniform presumption of the law of the land; a presumption which is always allowed freely and fully to operate, until the fact is shown to be otherwise, by the party who denies the applicability of this presumption to the particular case in question. Whenever an objection is raised in opposition to ordinary presumptions of law, or to the ordinary experience of mankind, the burden of proof is devolved on the objector by the common and ordinary rules of evidence, and of practice in courts. No lawyer is permitted to argue in disparagement of the intelligence or integrity of a witness, against whom the case itself afforded no particle of testimony. This is sufficient for our purpose, in regard to these witnesses. But more than this is evident, from the minuteness of their narrative, and from their history. Matthew was trained, by his calling, to habits of severe investigation and suspicious scrutiny; Luke's profession demanded an exactness of observation equally close and searching. The other two evangelists, it has been well remarked, were as much too unlearned to forge the story of their master's life, as these were too learned and acute to be deceived by any imposture.

§ 34. In the *third* place, as to their *number* and the *consistency* of their testimony. The character of their narratives is like that of all other true witnesses, containing, as Dr. Paley observes, substantial truth, under circumstantial variety. There is enough of discrepancy to show that there could have been no previous concert among them, and at the same time such substantial agreement as to show that they all were independent narrators of the same great transaction, as the events actually occurred. That they conspired to impose falsehood upon the world is, moreover, utterly inconsistent with the supposition that they were honest men; a fact, to the proofs of which we have already adverted. But if they were bad men, still the idea of any conspiracy among them is negatived, not only by the discrepancies alluded to, but by many other circumstances which will be mentioned hereafter; from all which, it is manifest that if they concerted a false story, they sought its accomplishment by a mode quite the opposite to that which all others are found to pursue, to attain the same end. On this point the profound remark of an eminent writer is to dour purpose; that "in a number of concurrent testimonies, where there has been no previous concert, there is a probability distinct from that which may be termed the sum of the probabilities resulting from the testimonies of the witnesses; a probability which would remain, even though the witnesses were of such a character as to merit no faith at all. This probability arises from the concurrence itself. That such a concurrence should spring from chance is as one to infinite; that is, in other words, morally impossible. If therefore concert be excluded, there remains no cause but the reality of the fact."[55]

§ 35. The discrepancies between the narratives of the several evangelists, when carefully examined, will not be found sufficient to invalidate their testimony. Many seeming contradictions will prove, upon closer scrutiny, to be in substantial agreement; and it may be confidently asserted that there are none that will not yield, under fair and just criticism. If these different accounts of the same transactions were in strict verbal conformity with each other, the argument against their credibility would be much stronger. All that is asked for these witnesses is that their testimony may be regarded as we regard the testimony of men in the ordinary affairs of life. This they are justly entitled to; and this no honorable adversary can refuse. We might, indeed, take higher ground than this, and confidently claim for them the severest scrutiny; but our present purpose is merely to try their veracity by the ordinary tests of truth, admitted in human tribunals.

§ 36. If the evidence of the evangelists is to be rejected because of a few discrepancies among them, we shall be obliged to discard that of many of the contemporaneous histories on which we are accustomed to rely. Dr. Paley has noticed the contradiction between Lord Clarendon and Burnett and others in regard to Lord Strafford's execution: the former stating that he was condemned to be hanged, which was done on the same day and the latter all relating that on a Saturday he was sentenced to the block, and was beheaded on the following Monday. Another striking instance of discrepancy has since occurred, in the narratives of the different members of the royal family of France, of their flight from Paris to Varennes, in 1792. These narratives, ten in number, and by eye-witnesses and personal actions in the transactions they relate, contradict each other, some in trivial and some on more essential points, but in every case in a wonderful and inexplicable manner.[56] Yet these contradictions do not, in the general public estimation, detract from the integrity of the narrators, nor from the credibility of their relations. In the points in which they agree, and which constitute the great body of their narratives, their testimony is of course not doubted where they differ, we reconcile them, as well as we may; and where this cannot be done at all, we follow that light which seems to us the clearest. Upon the principles of the skeptic, we should be bound utterly to disbelieve them all. On the contrary, we apply to such cases the rules which, in daily experience, our judges instruct juries to apply, in weighing and reconciling the testimony of different witnesses; and which the courts themselves observe, in comparing and reconciling different and sometimes discordant reports of the same decisions. This remark applies especially to some alleged discrepancies in the reports which the several evangelists have given of the same discourses of our Lord.[57]

§ 37. In the *fourth* place, as to the *conformity of their testimony with experience.* The title of the evangelists to full credit for veracity would be readily conceded by the objector, if the facts they relate were such as ordinarily occur in human experience, and on this circumstance an argument is founded against their credibility. Miracles, say the objectors, are impossible; and therefore the evangelists were either deceivers or deceived and in either case their narratives are unworthy of belief. Spinosa's argument against the possibility of miracles was founded on the broad and bold assumption that all things are governed by immutable laws, or fixed modes of motion and relation, termed *the laws of nature,* by which God himself is of necessity bound. This erroneous assumption is the tortoise, on which stands the elephant which upholds his system of atheism. He does not inform us who made these immutable laws, nor whence they derive their binding force and irresistible operation. The argument supposes that the creator of all things first made a code of laws, and then put it out of his own power to change them. The scheme of Mr. Hume is but another form of the same error. He deduces the existence of such immutable laws from the uniform course of human experience. This, he affirms, is our only guide in reasoning concerning matters of fact; and whatever is contrary to human experience, he pronounces incredible.[58] Without stopping to examine the correctness of this doctrine as a fundamental principle in the law of evidence, it is sufficient in this place to remark that it contains this fallacy: it excludes all knowledge derived by inference or deduction from facts, confining us to what we derive from experience alone, and thus depriving us of any knowledge or even rational belief of the existence or character of God. Nay more, it goes to prove that successive generations of men can make no advancement in knowledge, but each must begin *de novo* and be limited to the results of his own experience. But if we may infer, from what we see and know, that there is a Supreme Being, by whom this world was created, we may certainly, and with equal reason, believe him capable of works which we have never yet known him to perform. We may fairly conclude that the power which was originally put forth to create the world is still constantly and without ceasing exerted to sustain it; and that the experienced connection between cause and effect is but the uniform and constantly active operation of the finger of God. Whether this uniformity of operation extends to things beyond the limits of our observation is a point we cannot certainly know. Its existence in all things that ordinarily concern us may be supposed to be ordained as conducive to our happiness; and if the belief in a revelation of peace and mercy from God is conducive to the happiness of man, it is not irrational to suppose that he would depart from his ordinary course of action in order to give it such attestations as should tend to secure that belief. "A miracle is improbable, when we can perceive no sufficient cause, in reference to his creatures, why the Deity should not vary his modes of operation; it ceases to be so, when such cause is assigned."[59]

§ 38. But the full discussion of the subject of miracles forms no part of the present design. Their credibility has been fully established, and the objections of skeptics most satisfactorily met and overthrown by the ablest writers of our own day, whose works are easily accessible.[60] Thus much, however, may here be remarked: that in almost every miracle related by the evangelists, the facts, separately taken, were plain, intelligible, transpiring in public, and about which no person of ordinary observation would be likely to mistake. Persons blind or crippled, who applied to Jesus for relief, were known to have been crippled or blind for many years; they came to be cured; he spoke to them; they went away whole. Lazarus had been dead and buried four days; Jesus called him to come forth from the grave; he immediately came forth, and was seen alive for a long time afterwards. In every case of healing, the previous condition of the sufferer was known to all; all saw his instantaneous restoration; all witnessed the act of Jesus in touching him, and heard his words.[61] All these, separately considered, were facts, plain and simple in their nature, easily seen and fully comprehended by persons of common capacity and observation. If they were separately testified to, by different witnesses of ordinary intelligence and integrity, in any court of justice, the jury would be bound to believe them; and a verdict, rendered contrary to the uncontradicted testimony of credible witnesses to any of these plain facts, separately taken, would be liable to be set aside, as a verdict against evidence. If one credible witness testified to the fact that Bartimeus was blind, according to the uniform course of administering justice, this fact would be taken as satisfactorily proved. So also, if his subsequent restoration to sight were the sole fact in question, this also would be deemed established, by the like evidence. Nor would the rule of evidence be at all different if the fact to be proved were the declaration of Jesus, immediately preceding his restoration to sight, that his faith had made him whole. In each of these cases, each isolated fact was capable of being accurately observed, and certainly known; and the evidence upon any other indifferent subject. The connection of the word or the act of Jesus with the restoration of the blind, lame, and dead to sight, health, and life, as cause and effect, is a conclusion which our reason is compelled to admit, from the uniformity of their concurrence, in such a multitude of instances, as well as from the universal conviction of all, whether friends or foes, who beheld the miracles which he wrought. Indeed, if the truth of one of the miracles is satisfactorily established, our belief cannot reasonably be withheld from them all. This is the issue proposed by Dr. Paley, in regard to the evidence of the death of Jesus upon the cross, and his subsequent resurrection, the truth of which he has established in an argument, incapable of refutation.

§ 39. In the *fifth* place, as to *the coincidence of their testimony, with collateral and contemporaneous facts and circumstances*. After a witness is dead and his moral character is forgotten, we can ascertain it only by a close inspection of his narrative, comparing its details with each other, and with contemporary accounts and collateral facts. This test is much more accurate than may at first be supposed. Every event which actually transpires has its appropriate relation and place in the vast complication of circumstances, of which the affairs of men consist; it owes its origin to the events which have preceded it, is intimately connected with all others which occur at the same time and place, and often with those of remote regions, and in its turn gives birth to numberless others which succeed. In all this almost inconceivable contexture, and seeming discord, there is perfect harmony; and while the fact, which really happened, tallies exactly with every other contemporaneous incident, related to it in the remotest degree, it is not possible for the wit of man to invent a story, which, if closely compared with the actual occurrences of the same time and place, may not be shown to be false.[62] Hence it is, that a false witness will not willingly detail any circumstances in which his testimony will be open to contradiction, nor multiply them where there is danger of his being detected by a comparison of them with other accounts, equally circumstantial. He will rather deal in general statements and broad assertions, and if he finds it necessary for his purpose to employ names and particular circumstances in his story, he will endeavor to invent such as shall be out of the reach of all opposing proof; and he will be the most forward and minute in details, where he knows that any danger of contradiction is least to be apprehended.[63] Therefore it is, that variety and minuteness of detail are usually regarded as certain test of sincerity, if the story, in the circumstances related, is of a nature capable of easy refutation if it were false.

§ 40. The difference, in the detail of circumstances, between artful or false witnesses and those who testify the truth, is worthy of especial observation. The former are often copious and even profuse in their statements, as far as these may have been previously fabricated, and in relation to the principal matter; but beyond this, all will be reserved and meagre, from the fear of detection. Every lawyer knows how lightly the evidence of a *non-mi-recordo* witness is esteemed. The testimony of false witnesses will not be uniform in its texture, but will be unequal, unnatural, and inconsistent. On the contrary, in the testimony of true witnesses there is a visible and striking naturalness of manner, and an unaffected readiness and copiousness in the detail of circumstances, as well in one part of the narrative as another, and evidently without the least regard either to the facility or difficulty of verification or detection.[64] It is easier, therefore, to make out the proof of any fact, if proof it may be called, by suborning one or more false witnesses to testify directly to the matter in question, than to procure an equal number to testify falsely to such collateral and separate circumstances as will, without greater danger of detection, lead to the same false result. The increased number of witnesses to circumstances, and the increased number of the circumstances themselves, all tend to increase the probability of detection if the witnesses are false, because thereby the points are multiplied in which their statements may be compared with each other, as well as with the truth itself, and in the same proportion is increased the danger of variance and inconsistency.[65] Thus the force of circumstantial evidence is found to depend on the number of particulars involved in the narrative; the difficulty of fabricating them all, if false, and the great facility of detection; the nature of the circumstances to be compared, and from which the dates and other facts are to be collected; the intricacy of the comparison; the number of the intermediate steps in the process of deduction; and the circuity of the investigation. The more largely the narrative partake of these characters, the further it will be found removed from all suspicion of contrivance or design, and the more profoundly the mind will repose on the conviction of its truth.

§ 41. The narratives of the sacred writers, both Jewish and Christian, abound in examples of this kind of evidence, the value of which is hardly capable of being properly estimated. It does not, as has been already remarked, amount to mathematical demonstration; nor is this degree of proof justly demandable in any question of moral conduct. In all human transactions, the highest degree of assurance to which we can arrive, short of the evidence of our own senses, is that of probability. The most that can be asserted is that the narrative is more likely to be true than false; and it may be in the highest degree more likely, but still be short of absolute mathematical certainty. Yet this very probability may be so great as to satisfy the mind of the most cautious, and enforce the assent of the most reluctant and unbelieving. If it is such as usually satisfies reasonable men, in matters of ordinary transaction, it is all which the greatest skeptic has a right to require; for it is by such evidence alone that our rights are determined in the civil tribunals; and on no other evidence do they proceed, even in capital cases. Thus where a house had been feloniously broken open with a knife, the blade of which was broken and left in the window, and the mutilated knife itself, the parts perfectly agreeing, was found in the pocket of the accused, who gave no satisfactory explanation of the fact, no reasonable doubt remained of his participation in the crime. And where a murder had been committed by shooting with a pistol, and the prisoner was connected with the transaction by proof that the wadding of the pistol was part of a letter addressed to him, the remainder of which was found upon his person, no juror's conscience could have reproached him for assenting to the verdict of condemnation.[66] Yet the evidence, in both cases, is but the evidence of circumstances, amounting, it is true, to the highest degree of probability, but yet not utterly inconsistent with the innocence of the accused. The evidence which we have of the great facts of the Bible history belongs to this class, that is, it is moral evidence; sufficient to satisfy any rational mind, by carrying it to the highest degree of moral certainty. If such evidence well justify the taking away of human life or liberty, in the one case, surely it ought to be deemed sufficient to determine our faith in the other.

§ 42. All that Christianity asks of men on this subject is that they would be consistent with themselves; that they would treat its evidences as they threat the evidence of other things; and that they would try and judge its actors and witnesses as they deal with their fellow men, when testifying to human affairs and actions, in human tribunals. Let the witnesses be compared with themselves, with each other, and with surrounding facts and circumstances; and let their testimony be sifted, as if it were given in a court of justice, on the side of the adverse party, the witness being subjected to a rigorous cross-examination. The result, it is confidently believed, will be an undoubting conviction of their integrity, ability, and truth. In the course of such an examination, the undesigned concidences will multiply upon us at every step in our progress; the probability or the veracity of the witnesses and of the reality of the occurrences which they relate will increase, until it acquires, for all practical purposes, the value and force of demonstration.

§ 43. It should be remembered that very little of the literature of their times and country has come down to us, and that the collateral sources and means of corroborating and explaining their writings are proportionally limited. The contemporary writings and works of art which have reached us have invariably been found to confirm their accounts, to reconcile what was apparently contradictory, and supply what seemed defective or imperfect. We ought therefore to conclude that if we had more of the same light, all other similar difficulties and imperfections would vanish. Indeed they have been gradually vanishing, and rapidly too, before the light of modern research, conducted by men of science in our own times. And it is worthy of remark that of all the investigations and discoveries of travelers and men of letters, since the overthrow of the Roman empire, not a vestige of antiquity has been found impeaching, in the slightest degree, the credibility of the sacred writers; but on the contrary, every result has tended to confirm it.

§ 44. The essential marks of difference between true narratives of facts and the creations of fiction have already been adverted to. It may here be added that these attributes of truth are strikingly apparent throughout the gospel histories, and that the absence of all the others is equally remarkable. The writers allude, for example, to the existing manners and customs, and to the circumstances of the times and of their country. with the utmost minuteness of reference. And these references are never formally made, nor with preface and explanation, never multiplied and heaped on each other, nor brought together, as though introduced by design; but they are scattered broadcast and singly over every part of the story, and so connect themselves with every incident related as to render the detection of falsehood inevitable. This minuteness, too, is not peculiar to any one of the historians, but is common to them all. Though they wrote at different periods and without mutual concert, they all alike refer incidentally to the same state of affairs, and to the same contemporary and collateral circumstances. Their testimony, in this view, stands on the same ground with that of four witnesses, separately examined before different commissioners, upon the same interrogatories, and all adverting incidentally to the same circumstances as surrounding and accompanying the principal transaction, to which alone their attention is directed. And it is worthy of observation that these circumstances were at that time of a peculiar character. Hardly a state or kingdom in the world ever experienced so many vicissitudes in its government and political relations as did Judea, during the period of the gospel history. It was successively under the government of Herod the Great, of Archelaus, and of a Roman magistrate; it was a kingdom, a tetrarchate, and a province; and its affairs, its laws, and the administration of justice, were all involved in the confusion and uncertainty naturally to be expected from recent conquest. It would be difficult to select any place or period in the history of nations, for the time and scene of a fictitious history or an imposture, which would combine so many difficulties for the fabricator to surmount, so many contemporary writers to confront with him, and so many facilities for the detection of falsehood.[67]

§ 45. "Had the evangelists been false historians," says Dr. Chalmers, "they would not have committed themselves upon so many particulars. They would not have furnished the vigilant inquirers of that period with such an effectual instrument for bringing them into discredit with the people; nor foolishly supplied, in every page of their narrative, so many materials for a cross-examination, which would infallibly have disgraced them. Now, we of this age can institute the same cross-examination. We can compare the evangelical writers with contemporary authors, and verify a number of circumstances in the history, and government, and peculiar economy of the Jewish people. We therefore have it in our power to institute as cross-examination upon the writers of the New Testament; and the freedom and frequency of their allusions to these circumstances supply us with ample materials for it. The fact, that they are borne out in their minute and incidental allusions by the testimony of other historians, gives a strong weight of what has been called circumstantial evidence in their favor. As a specimen of the argument, let us confine our observations to the history of our Savior's trial, and execution, and burial. They brought him to Pontius Pilate. We know both from Tacitus and Josephus, that he was at that time governor of Judea. A sentence from him was necessary before they could proceed to the execution of Jesus; and we know that the power of life and death was usually vested in the Roman governor. Our Savior was treated with derision; and this we know to have been a customary practice at that time, previous to the execution of criminals, and during the time of it. Pilate scourged Jesus before he gave him up to be crucified. We know from ancient authors, that this was a very usual practice among Romans. The accounts of an execution generally run in this form: he was stripped, whipped, and beheaded or executed. According to the evangelists, his accusation was written on the top of the cross; and we learn from Suetonius and others, that the crime of the person to be executed was affixed to the instrument of his punishment. According to the evangelists, this accusation was written in three different languages; and we know from Josephus that it was quite common in Jerusalem to have all public advertisements written in this manner. According to the evangelists, Jesus had to bear his cross; and we know form other sources of information, that this was the constant practice of these times. According to the evangelists, the body of Jesus was given up to be buried at the request of friends. We know that, unless the criminal was infamous, this was the law or the custom with all Roman governors."[68]

§ 46. There is also a striking naturalness in the characters exhibited in the sacred historians, rarely if ever found in works of fiction, and probably nowhere else to be collected in a similar manner from fragmentary and incidental allusions and expressions, in the writing of different persons. Take, for example, that of Peter, as it may be gathered from the evangelists, and it will be hardly possible to conceive that four persons, writing at different times, could have concurred in the delineation of such a character, if it were not real; a character too, we must observe, which is nowhere expressly drawn, but is shown only here and there, casually, in the subordinate parts of the main narrative. Thus disclosed, it is that of a confident, sanguine, and zealous man; sudden and impulsive, yet humble and ready to retract; honest and direct in his purposes; ardently loving his master, yet deficient in fortitude and firmness in the cause.[69] When Jesus put any question to the apostles, it was Peter who was foremost to reply;[70] and if they would inquire of Jesus, it was Peter who was readiest to speak.[71] He had the impetuous courage to cut off the ear of the high priest's servant, who came to arrest his master; and the weakness to dissemble before the Jews, in the matter of eating with Gentile converts.[72] It was he who ran with John to the sepulcher on the first intelligence of the resurrection of Jesus, and with characteristic zeal rushed in, while John paused outside the door.[73] He had the ardor to desire and the faith to attempt to walk on the water at the command of his Lord; but as soon as he saw the wind boisterous, he was afraid.[74] He was the first to propose the election of another apostle in the place of Judas;[75] and he it was who courageously defended them all on the day of Pentecost, when the multitude charged them with being filled with new wine.[76] He was forward to acknowledge Jesus to be the Messiah;[77] yet having afterwards endangered his own life by wounding the servant of the high priest, he suddenly consulted his own safety by denying the same Master for whom, but a few hours before, he had declared himself ready to die.[78] We may safely affirm that the annals of fiction afford no example of a similar but not uncommon character, thus incidentally delineated.

§ 47. There are other internal marks of truth in the narratives of the evangelists, which, however, need here be only alluded to, as they have been treated with great fullness and force by able writers, whose works are familiar to all.[79] Among these may be mentioned the nakedness of the narratives; the absence of all parade by the writers about their own integrity, of all anxiety to be believed, or to impress others with a good opinion of themselves or their cause, of all marks of wonder, or of desire to excite astonishment at the greatness of the events they record, and of all appearance of design to exalt their master. On the contrary, there is apparently the most perfect indifference on their part whether they are believed or not; or rather, the evident consciousness that they are recording events well known to all in their own country and times, and undoubtedly to be believed, like any other matter of public history, by readers in all other countries and ages. It is worthy, too, of especial observation that though the evangelists record the unparalleled sufferings and cruel death of their beloved Lord, and this too, by hands and with the consenting voices of those on whom he had conferred the greatest benefits, and their own persecutions and dangers, yet they have bestowed no epithets of harshness or even of just censure on the authors of all this wickedness, but have everywhere left the plain and unencumbered narrative to speak for itself, and the reader to pronounce his own sentence of condemnation; like true witnesses, who have nothing to gain or to lose by the event of the cause, they state the facts, and leave them to their fate. Their simplicity and artlessness, also, should not pass unnoticed, in readily stating even those things most disparaging to themselves. Their want of faith in their master, their dullness of apprehension of his teachings, their strifes for preeminence, their desertion of their Lord in his hour of extreme peril; these and many other incidents tending directly to their own dishonor are nevertheless set down with all the directness and sincerity of truth, as by men writing under the deepest sense of responsibility to God. Some of the more prominent instances of this class of proofs will be noticed hereafter, in their proper places, in the narratives themselves.

§ 48. Lastly, the great character they have portrayed is perfect. It is the character of a sinless Being, of one supremely wise and supremely good. It exhibits no error, no sinister intention, no imprudence, no ignorance, no evil passion, no impatience; in a word, no fault; but all is perfect uprightness, innocence, wisdom, goodness, and truth. The mind of man has never conceived the idea of such a character, even for his gods; nor has history or poetry shadowed it forth. The doctrines and precepts of Jesus are in strict accordance with the attributes of God, agreeably to the most exalted idea which we can form of them, either from reason or from revelation. They are strikingly adapted to the capacity of mankind, and yet are delivered with a simplicity and majesty wholly divine. He spake as never man spake. He spake with authority, yet addressed himself to the reason and the understanding of men; and he spake with wisdom, which men could neither deny nor resist. In his private life, he exhibits a character not merely of strict justice, but of overflowing benignity. He is temperate, without austerity; his meekness and humility are signal; his patience is invincible; truth and sincerity light up his whole conduct; every one of his virtues is regulated by consummate discernment; and he both wins the love of his friends, and extorts the wonder and admiration of his enemies.[80] He is represented in every variety of situation in life, from the height of worldly grandeur, amid the acclamations of an admiring multitude, to the deepest abyss of human degradation and woe, apparently deserted of God and man. Yet everywhere he is the same, displaying a character of unearthly perfection, symmetrical in all its proportions, and encircled with splendor more than human. Either the men of Galilee were men of superlative wisdom, and extensive knowledge and experience, and of deeper skill in the arts of deception than any and all others, before or after them, or they have truly stated the astonishing things which they saw and heard.

The narratives of the evangelists are now submitted to the reader's perusal and examination, upon the principles and by the rules already stated. For this purpose, and for the sake of more ready and close comparison, they are arranged in juxtaposition, after the general order of the latest and most approved harmonies. The question is not upon the strict propriety of the arrangement, but upon the veracity of the witnesses and the credibility of their narratives. With the relative merits of modern harmonists, and with points of controversy among theologians the writer has no concern. His business is that of a lawyer examining the testimony of witnesses by the rules of his profession, in order to ascertain whether, if they had thus testified on oath, in a court of justice, they would be entitled to credit and whether their narratives, as we now have them, would be received as ancient documents, coming from the proper custody. If so, then it is believed that every honest and impartial man will act consistently with that result, by receiving their testimony in all the extent of its import. To write out a full commentary or argument upon the text would be a useless addition to the bulk of the volume; but a few notes have been added for illustration of the narratives, and for the clearing up of apparent discrepancies, as being all that members of the legal profession would desire.

Notes

1. Nov. *Org.* 1.68. "Ut non alius fere sit aditus ad regnum hominis, quod fundatur in scientiis, quam ad regnum coelorum in quod, nisi sub persona infantis, intrare non datur."

2. Bishop Wilson, *Evidences of Christianity*, 1.38.

3. See Hopkins, *Lowell Lectures*, particularly Lect. 2. Wilson, *Evidences* 1.45–61. Horne, *Introduction to the Study of the Holy Scriptures* 1.1–39. Mr. Horne having cited all the best English writers on this subject, it is sufficient to refer to his work alone.

4. Hopkins, *Lowell Lectures*, p. 48.

5. It has been well remarked, that, if we regard man as in a state of innocence, we should naturally expect that God would hold communications with him; that if we regard him as guilty, and as having lost the knowledge and moral image of God, such a communication would be absolutely necessary, if man was to be restored. Hopkins, *Lowell Lectures,* p. 62.

6. The argument here briefly sketched is stated more at large, and with great clearness and force, in an essay entitled "The Philosophy of the Plan of Salvation," pp. 13–107.

7. See Stuart, *Critical History and Defense of the Old Testament Canon*, where this is abundantly proved.

8. Per Tindal Ch. J., in the case of *Bishop of Meath v Marquis of Winchester,* 3 Bing. N C 183, 200–201. "It is when documents are found in other than their proper places of deposit," observed the Chief Justice, "that the investigation commences, whether it was reasonable and natural, under the circumstances of the particular case, to expect that they should have been in the place where they are actually found for it is obvious, that, while there can be only one place of deposit strictly and absolutely proper, there may be many and various, that are reasonable and probable, though differing in degree, some being more so, some less; and in these cases the proposition to be determined is, whether the actual custody is so reasonably and probably accounted for, that it impresses the mind with the conviction that the instrument found in such custody must be genuine." See the cases cited in *Greenleaf on Evidence* § 142; see also 1 *Stark. on Ev.* pp. 332–335, 381–386; *Croughton v Blake*, 12 Mees. & W. 205, 208; *Doe v Phillips*, 10 Jur 34. It is this defect, namely, that they do not come from the proper or natural repository, which

shows the fabulous character of many pretended revelations, from the Gospel of the Infancy to the Book of Mormon.

9. *Greenl. on Ev.* §§ 34, 142, 570.

10. *Morewood v Wood*, 14 East, 329, n., per Lord Kenyon; *Weeks v Sparke*, 1 M. & S. 686; Berkeley Peerage Case, 4 Campb. 416, per Mansfield, Ch. J.; see 1 *Greenl. on Ev.* § 128.

11. 1 *Stark. on Ev.* 195, 230; 2 *Greenl. on Ev.* § 483.

12. The arguments for the genuineness and authenticity of the books of the Holy Scriptures are briefly, yet very fully stated, and almost all the writers of authority are referred in Horne, *Introduction* vol. 1, passim. The same subject is discussed in a more popular manner in the *Lectures* of Bishop Wilson, and of Bishop Sumner of Chester, on the *Evidences of Christianity;* and, in America, the same question, as it relates to the Gospels, has been argued by Bishop McIlvaine, in his *Lectures.*

13. See the case of the Slane Peerage, 5 Clark & F. 24. See also the case of the Fitzwalter Peerage, 10 Id. 948.

14. Matt. 9:10; Mark 2:14–15; Luke 5:29.

15. The authorities on this subject are collected in Horne, *Introduction* 4.234–238, part 2 chap. 2 Sec. 2.

16. See Horne, *Introduction* 4.229–232.

17. See Campbell on the *Four Gospels* 3.35–36; Preface to Matthew's Gospel, §§ 22–23.

18. See Gibbon, *Rome* vol. 1 chap. 6 and vol. 3 chap. 17 and authorities there cited. Cod. Thoed. Lib. xi:tit. 1–28, with the notes of Gothofred. Gibbon treats particularly of the revenues of a latter period than our Savior's time; but the general course of proceeding, in the levy and collection of taxes, is not known to have been changed since the beginning of the empire.

19. Acts 12:12, 25; 13:5, 13; and 15:36–41; 2 Tim. 4:11; Philem. 24; Col. 4:10; 1 Pet. 5:13.

20. Horne, *Introduction* 4.252–253.

21. Mark 7:2, 11; 9:43, and elsewhere.

22. Mr. Norton has conclusively disposed of this objection, in his *Evidences of the Genuineness of the Gospels*, vol. 1 Additional Notes, sec. 2, pp. 115–132.

23. Compare Mark 10:46; 14:69; 4:35; 1:35; 9:28, with Matthew's narrative of the same events.

24. See Horne, *Introduction* 4.252–259.

25. Acts 16:10–11.

26. Col. 4:14. Luke, the beloved physician.

27. Luke 5:12; Matt. 8:2; Mark 1:40.

28. Luke 6:6; Matt. 12:10; Mark 3:1.

29. Luke 8:55; Matt. 9:25; Mark 5:42.

30. Luke 6:19.

31. Luke 22:44–45, 51.

32. See Horne, *Introduction* 4.260–272, where references may be found to earlier writers.

33. See Lardner, *Works* 6.138–139; 3.203–204; and other authors, cited in Horne, *Introduction* 1.267.

34. 2 *Phil. on Ev.* p. 95 (9th edition).

35. When Abbot, Archbishop of Canterbury, in shooting a deer with a crossbow, in Bramsil park, accidentally killed the keeper, King James I by a letter dated Oct. 3, 1621, requested the Lord Keeper, the Lord Chief Justice, and others, to inquire into the circumstances and consider the case and "the scandal that may have risen thereupon." and to certify the King what it may amount to. Could there be any reasonable doubt of their report of the facts, thus ascertained? See Spelman, *Posthumous Works*, p. 121.

36. The case of the ill-fated steamer *President* furnishes an example of this sort of inquiry. This vessel, it is well known, sailed from New York for London in the month of March, 1841, having on board many passengers, some of whom were highly connected. The ship was soon overtaken by a storm, after which she was never heard of. A few months afterwards a solemn inquiry was instituted by three gentlemen of respectability, one of whom was a British admiral, another was agent for the underwriters at Lloyd's, and the other a government packet agent, concerning the time, circumstances, and causes of that disaster; the result of which was communicated to the public, under their hands. This document received universal confidence, and no further inquiry was made.

37. Mark. 1:20.

38. John 19:26–27.

39. John 13:23.

40. Matt. 27:55–56; Mark 15:40–41.

41. John 18:15–16.

42. Luke 8:51; Matt. 17:1; 26:37.

43. This account is abridged from Horne, *Introduction* 4.286–288.

44. Horne, *Introduction* 4.289, and authors there cited.

45. See, among others, John 1:38, 41; 2:6, 13; 4:9; 11:55.

46. See Horne, *Introduction* 4.297–298.

47. See Gambier, *Guide to the Study of Moral Evidence,* p. 121.

48. 1 *Stark. on Evidence.* pp. 514, 577; 1 *Greenl. on Evidence.* §§1–2; Willis, *Circumstantial Evidence* p. 2; Whately, *Logic* bk. 4 ch. 3 § 1.

49. See 1 *Stark. on Evidence.* pp. 16, 480, 521.

50. This subject has been treated by Dr. Chalmers, in his *Evidences of the Christian Revelation*, chapter 3. The following extract from his observations will not be unacceptable to the reader. "In other cases, when we compare the

narratives of contemporary historians, it is not expected that all the circumstances alluded to by one will be taken notice of by the rest; and it often happens that an event or a custom is admitted upon the faith of a single historian; and the silence of all other writers is not suffered to attach suspicion or discredit to his testimony. It is an allowed principle, that a scrupulous resemblance between two histories is very far from necessary to their being held consistent with one another. And what is more, it sometimes happens that, with contemporary historians, there may be an apparent contradiction, and the credit of both parties remain as entire and unsuspicious as before. Posterity is, in these cases, disposed to make the most liberal allowances. Instead of calling it a contradiction, they often call it a difficulty. They are sensible that, in many instances a seeming variety of statement has, upon a more extensive knowledge of ancient history, admitted of a perfect reconciliation. Instead, then, of referring the difficulty in question to the inaccuracy or bad faith of any of the parties, they, with more justness and more modesty, refer it to their own ignorance, and to that obscurity which necessarily hangs over the history of every remote age. These principles are suffered to have great influence in every secular investigation; but so soon as, instead of a secular, it becomes a sacred investigation, every ordinary principle is abandoned, and the suspicion annexed to the teachers of religion is carried to the dereliction of all that candor and liberality with which every other document of antiquity is judged of and appreciated. How does it happen that the authority of Josephus should be acquiesced in as a first principle, while every step, in the narrative of the evangelists, must have foreign testimony to confirm and support it? How comes it that the silence of Josephus should be construed into an impeachment of the testimony of the evangelists, while it is never admitted, for a single moment, that the silence of the evangelists, can impart the slightest blemish to the testimony of Josephus? How comes it, that the supposition of two Philips in one family should throw a damp of skepticism over the Gospel narrative, while the only circumstance which renders that supposition necessary is the single testimony of Josephus; in which very testimony it is necessarily implied that there are two Herods in that same family? How comes it, that the evangelists, with as much internal, and a vast deal more of external evidence in their favor, should be made to stand before Josephus, like so many prisoners at the bar of justice? In any other case, we are convinced that this would be looked upon as *rough handling*. But we are not sorry for it. It has given more triumph and confidence to the argument. And it is no small addition to our faith, that its first teachers have survived an examination, which, in point of rigor and severity, we believe to be quite unexampled in the annals of criticism." See Chalmer, *Evidences*, pp. 72–74.

51. See 1 *Stark. on Ev.* pp. 480, 545.

52. If the witnesses could be supposed to have been biased, this would not

destroy their testimony to matters of fact; it would only detract from the weight of their judgment in matters of opinion. The rule of law on this subject has been thus stated by Dr. Lushington: "When you examine the testimony of witnesses nearly connected with the parties, and there is nothing very peculiar tending to destroy their credit, when they depose to mere facts, their testimony is to be believed; when they depose as to matter of opinion, it is to be received with suspicion." *Dillon v Dillon*, 3 Curteis, *Eccl. Rep.* pp. 96, 102.

53. This subject has been so fully treated by Dr. Paley, in his view of the *Evidences of Christianity*, Part 1, Prop. 1, that it is unnecessary to pursue it farther in this place.

54. 1 *Stark. on Ev.* pp. 483, 548.

55. Campbell, *Philosophy of Rhetoric*, c. v. b. 1. Part 3, p. 125; Whately, *Rhetoric*, part 1. ch. 2 § 4; 1 *Stark. on Ev.* p. 487.

56. See the *Quarterly Review*, 28:465. These narrators were, the Duchess D'Angouleme herself, the two Messrs. De Bouille, the Duc De Choiseul, his servant, James Briaasc, Messrs. De Damas and Deslons, two of the officers commanding detachments on the road, Messrs. De Moustier and Valori, the garde du corps who accompanied the king, and finally M. de Fontanges, archbishop of Toulouse, who though not himself a party to the transaction, is supposed to have written from the information of the queen. An earlier instance in similar discrepancy is mentioned by Sully. After the battle of Aumale, in which Henry IV was wounded, when the officers were around the king's bed, conversing upon the events of the day, there were not two who agreed in the recital of the most particular circumstance of the action. D'Aubigne, a contemporary writer, does not even mention the king's wound, though it was the only one he ever received in his life. See Memoirs in Sully, 1:245. If we treated these narratives as skeptics would have us treat those of the sacred writers, what evidence should we have of any battle at Aumale, or of any flight to Varennes?

57. Far greater discrepancies can be found in the different reports of the same case, given by the reporters of legal judgments than are shown among the evangelists; and yet we do not consider them detracting from the credit of the reporters, to whom we still report with confidence, as to good authority. Some of these discrepancies seem utterly irreconcilable. Thus in a case, 45 Edv. 3:19, where the question was upon a gift of lands to J. de C. with Joan, the sister of the donor, and to their heirs, Fitzherbert (tit. *Tail*, 14) says it was adjudged fee simple, and not frankmarriage; Statham (tit. *Tail*) says it was adjudged a gift in frankmarriage; while Brook (tit. *Frankmarriage*) says it was not decided. Vid. 10 Co. 118. Others are irreconcilable, until the aid of a third reporter is invoked. Thus, in the case of *Cooper v Franklin*, Croke says it was not decided, but adjourned (Cro. Jac. 100) Godbolt says it was decided

in a certain way, which he mentions (Godb. 269); Moor also reports it as decided, but gives a different account of the question raised (Moor, 848): while Bulstrode gives a still different report of the judgment of the court, which he says was delivered by Croke himself. But by his account it further appears that the case was previously twice argued; and thus it at length results that the other reporters relate only what fell from the court on each of the previous occasions. Other similar examples may be found in 1 Dougl. 6, n. compared with 5 East, 475, n. in the case of *Galbraith v Neville*; and in that of *Stoughton v Reynolds*, reported by Fortescue, Strange, and in Cases temp. Hardwicke. See 3 Barn. & A. 247–248. Indeed, the books abound in such instances. Other discrepancies are found in the names of the same litigating parties, as differently given by reporters; such as *Putt v Roster,* 2 Mod. 318; *Foot v Rastall*, Skin. 49, and *Putt v Royston*, 2 Show. 211; also, *Hosdell v Harris*, 2 Keb. 462; *Hodson v Harwich*, Ib. 533, and *Hodsden v Harridge,* 2 Saund. 64, and a multitude of others, which are universally admitted to mean the same cases, even when they are not precisely within the rule of *idem sonans*. These diversities, it is well known, have never detracted in the slightest degree from the estimation in which the reporters are all deservedly held, as authors of merit, enjoying, to this day the confidence of the profession. Admitting now for the sake of argument (what is not conceded in fact), that diversities equally great exist among the sacred writers, how can we consistently, and as lawyers, raise any serious objection against them on that account, or treat them in any manner different from that which we observe towards our reporters?

58. Mr. Hume's argument is thus refuted by Lord Brougham. "Here are two answers, to which the doctrine proposed by Mr. Hume is exposed, and either appears sufficient to shake it.

"*First*—Our belief in the uniformity of the laws of nature rests not altogether upon an experience. We believe no man ever was raised from the dead,—not merely because we ourselves never saw it, for indeed that would be a very limited ground of deduction; and our belief was fixed on the subject long before we had any considerable experience,—fixed chiefly by authority,—that is, by deference to other men's experience. We found our confident belief in this negative position partly, perhaps chiefly, upon the testimony of others; and at all events, our belief that in times before our own the same position held good, must of necessity be drawn from our trusting the relations of other men—that is, it depends upon the evidence of testimony. If, then, the existence of the law of nature is proved, in great part at least, by such evidence, can we wholly reject the like evidence when it comes to prove an exception to the rule—a deviation from the law? The more numerous are the cases of the law being kept—the more rare those of its being broken—the more scrupulous certainly ought we to be in admitting the proofs of the breach. But that testimony is capable of making good the proof there seems no doubt. In truth, the degree of excellence and of strength to which testimony may arise seems almost indefinite. There is hardly any cogency which it is not capable by possible supposition of attaining. The endless multiplication of witnesses,—the unbounded variety of their habits of thinking, their prejudices, their interests,—afford the means of conceiving the force of their testimony, augmented *ad infinitum*, because these circumstances afford the means of diminishing indefinitely the chances of their being all mistaken, all mislead, or all combining to deceive us. Let any man try to calculate the chances of a thousand persons who come from different quarters, and never saw each other before, and who all vary in their habits, stations, opinions, interests,—being mistaken or combining to deceive us, when they give the same account of an event as having happened before their eyes,—these chances are many hundreds of thousands to one. And yet we can conceive them multiplied indefinitely; for one hundred thousand such witnesses may all in like manner bear the same testimony; and they may all tell us their story within twenty-four hours after the transaction, and in the next parish. And yet according to Mr. Hume's argument, we are bound to disbelieve them all, because they speak to a thing contrary our own experience, and to the accounts which other witnesses had formerly given us of the laws of nature, and which our forefathers had handed down to us as derived from witnesses who lived in the old time before them. It is unnecessary to add that no testimony of the witnesses, whom we are supposing to concur in their relation, contradicts any testimony of our own senses. If it did, the argument would resemble Archbishop Tillotson's upon the Real Presence, and our disbelief would be at once warranted.

"*Secondly*—This leads us to the next objection to which Mr. Hume's argument is liable, and which we have in part anticipated while illustrating the first. He requires us to withhold our belief in circumstances which would force every man of common understanding to lend his assent, and to act upon the supposition of the story told being true. For, suppose either such numbers of various witnesses as we have spoken of; or, what is perhaps stronger, suppose a miracle reported to us, first by a number of relators, and then by three or four of the very soundest judges and most incorruptibly honest men we know,—men noted for their difficult belief of wonders, and, above all, steady unbelievers in miracles, without any bias in favor of religion, but rather accustomed to doubt, if not disbelieve,— most people would lend an easy belief to any miracle thus vouched. But let us add this circumstance, that a friend on his death-bed had been attended by us, and that we had told him a fact known only to ourselves, something that we had secretly done the very moment before we told it to the dying man, and which to no other being we had ever revealed,— and that the credible witnesses we are supposing, informed us that the deceased appeared to them, conversed with them, and remained with them a day or two, accompanying them, and to avouch the fact of his reappearance on this earth, communicated to them the secret of which we had made him the sole depository the moment before his death;—according to Mr. Hume, we are bound rather to believe, not only that those credible witnesses deceived us, or that those sound and unprejudiced men were themselves deceived, and fancied things without real existence, but further, that they all hit by chance upon the discovery of a real secret, known only to ourselves and the dead man. Mr. Hume's argument requires us to believe this as the lesser improbability of the two—as less unlikely than the rising of one from the dead; and yet every one must feel convinced, that were he placed in the situation we have been figuring, he would not only lend his belief to the relation, but if the relators accompanied it with a special warning from the deceased person to avoid a certain contemplated act, he would, acting upon the belief of their story, take the warning, and avoid doing the forbidden deed. Mr. Hume's argument makes no exception. This is its scope; and whether he chooses to push it thus for or no, all miracles are of necessity denied by it, without the least regard to the kind or the quantity of the proof on which they are rested; and the testimony which we have supposed, accompanied by the test or check we have supposed, would fall within the grasp of the argument just as much and as clearly as any other miracle avouched by more ordinary combinations of evidence.

"The use of Mr. Hume's argument is this, and it is an important and a valuable one. It teaches us to sift closely and vigorously the evidence for miraculous events. It bids us remember that the probabilities are always, and must always be incomparably greater against, than for, the truth of these relations, because it is always far more likely that the testimony should be mistaken or false, than that the general laws of nature should be suspended. Further than this the doctrine cannot in soundness of reason be carried. It does not go the length of proving that those general laws cannot, by the force of human testimony, be shown to have been, in a particular instance, and with a particular purpose, suspended." See Brougham, *Discourse of Natural Theology*, Note 5, p. 210–214, ed. 1835.

Laplace, in his *Essai sur les Probabilities,* maintains that, the more extraordinary the fact attested, the greater the probability of error or falsehood in the attestor. Simple good sense, he says, suggests this; and the calculation of probabilities confirms its suggestion. These are some things, he adds, so extraordinary, that nothing can balance their improbability. The position here laid down is, that the probability of error, or the falsehood of testimony, becomes *in proportion* greater, as the fact which is attested is more extraordinary. And hence a fact extraordinary in the highest possible degree, becomes in the highest possible degree improbable; or so much so, that nothing can counterbalance its improbability.

This argument has been made much use of to discredit the evidence of miracles, and the truth of that divine religion which is attested by them. But however sound it may be, in one sense, this application of it is fallacious. The fallacy lies in the meaning affixed to the term *extraordinary*. If Laplace means a fact extraordinary *under* its existing circumstances and relations, that is, a fact remaining extraordinary, notwithstanding all its circumstances, the position needs not here to be controverted. But if the term means extraordinary *in the abstract*, it is far from bring universally true, or affording a correct test of truth, or rule of evidence. Thus, it is extraordinary that a man should leap fifteen feet at a bound; but not extraordinary that a strong and active man should do it, under a sudden impulse to save his life. The former is improbable in the abstract; the latter is rendered probable by the circumstances. So, things extraordinary, and therefore improbable under one hypothesis, become the reverse under another. Thus, the occurrence of a violent storm at sea, and the utterance by Jesus of the words, "Peace, be still," succeeded instantly by a perfect calm, are facts which, taken separately from each other, are not in themselves extraordinary. The connection between the command of Jesus and the ensuing calm, as cause and effect, would be extraordinary and improbable if he were a mere man; but it becomes perfectly natural and probable, when his divine power is considered. Each of those facts is in its nature so simple and obvious, that the most ignorant person is capable of observing it. There is nothing extraordinary in the facts themselves; and the extraordinary coincidence, in which the miracle consists, becomes both intelligible and probable upon the hypothesis of the Christian. See the *Christian Observer* for Oct, 1838, p. 617. The theory of Laplace may, with the same propriety, be applied to the creation of the world. That matter was created out of nothing is extremely improbable, in the abstract, that is, if there is no God; and therefore it is not to be believed. But if the existence of a Supreme Being is conceded, the fact is perfectly credible.

Laplace was so fascinated with his theory that he thought the calculus of probabilities might be usefully employed in discovering the value of different methods resorted to, in those sciences which are in a great measure conjectural, as medicine, agriculture, and political economy. And he proposed that there should be kept, in every branch of the administration, an exact register of the trials made of different measures, and of the results, whether good or bad, to which they have led. See the *Edinburgh Review*, 23:335–336. Napoleon, who appointed him Minister of the Interior, has thus described him: "A geometrician of the first class, he did not reach mediocrity as a statesman. He never viewed any subject in its true light; he was always occupied with subtleties; his notions were all problematic; and he carried into the administration the spirit of the *infinitely small.*" See the *Encyclopedia Britannica,* "Laplace"; *Memoires Ecrits a Ste. Helena,* 1:3. The injurious effect of deductive reasoning, upon the minds of those who addict themselves to this method alone, to the exclusion of all other modes of arriving at the knowledge of truth in fact, is shown with great clearness and success, by Mr. Whewel, in the ninth of the *Bridgwater Treatises,* book 3, ch 6. The calculus of probabilities has been applied by some writers to judicial evidence; but its very slight value as a test, is clearly shown in an able article on "Presumptive Evidence," in the *Law Magazine,* 1:28–32 (New Series).

59. See Norton, "Discourse on the latest form of Infidelity," p. 18.

60. The arguments on this subject are stated in a condensed form, by Horne, *Introduction to the Study of the Holy Scriptures,* vol. 1 chap. 4, sec. 2; in which he refers, among others, to Gregory, *Letters on the Evidences of the Christian Revelation;* Campbell, *Dissertation on Miracles;* Vince, *Sermons on the Credibility of Miracles;* Bishop Marsh, *Lectures,* part 6, lect. 30; Adams, *Treatise in reply to Mr. Hume;* Bishop Gleig, *Dissertation on Miracles,* (in the third volume of his edition of Stackhouse, *History of the Bible,* p. 240, etc.); Key, *Norissian Lectures,* vol. 1. See also Howell, *Lectures,* lect. 1–2 delivered in Boston in 1844, where this topic is treated with great perspicuity and cogency.

Among the more popular treaties on miracles, are Bogue, *Essay on the Divine Authority of the New Testament,* chap. 5; Wilson, *Evidences of Christianity,* vol. 1 lect. 7; Sumner, *Evidences,* chap. 10; Gambier, *Guide to the Study of Moral Evidence,* chap. 5; Norton, *Discourse on the latest form of Infidelity,* and Dewey, *Dudleian Lecture,* delivered before Harvard University, in May, 1836.

61. See Wilson, *Evidences,* lect 7, p. 130.

62. 1 *Stark. on Ev.* p. 496–499.

63. 1 *Stark. on Ev.* p. 523.

64. 1 *Stark. on Ev.* p. 487. The Gospels abound in instances of this. See, for example, Mark 15:21; John 18:10; Luke 23:6; Matt. 27:58–60; John 11:1.

65. 1 *Stark. on Ev.* pp. 522, 585.

66. See 1 *Stark. on Ev.* p. 498. *Wills on Circumstantial Evidence,* pp. 128–129.

67. See Chalmers, *Evidence,* chap. 3.

68. See Chalmers, *Evidence,* pp. 76–78, Amer. ed. Proofs of this kind copiously referred to by Mr. Horne, in his *Introduction,* &c. vol. 1, chap. 3, sect. 2:2.

69. See Mark 8:32; 9:5; 14:29; Matt. 16:22; 17:5; Luke 9:33; 18:18; John 13:8; 18:15.

70. Mark 8:29; Matt. 16:16; Luke 9:20.

71. Matt. 18:21; 19:27; John 13:36.

72. Gal. 2:11.
73. John 20:3–6.
74. Matt. 14:30.
75. Acts 1:15.
76. Acts 2:14.
77. Matt. 16:16; Mark 8:29; Luke 9:20; John 6:69.
78. Matt. 26:33, 35; Mark 14:29.
79. See Paley, *View of the Evidences of Christianity,* part 2 chap. 3–7; part 3 chap. 1; Chalmers, *Evidence and Authority of the Christian Revelation,* chap. 3–4, 8; Wilson, *Evidences of Christianity,* lect. 6; Bogue, *Essay on the Divine Authority of the New Testament,* chap. 3–4.
80. See Bogue, *Essay,* chap. 1 sec 2; Newcome's *Obs.* part 2 chap. 1 sec. 14.

An Account of the Trial of Jesus

by Simon Greenleaf

The death of Jesus is universally regarded among Christians as a cruel murder, perpetrated under the pretense of a legal sentence, after a trial, in which the forms of law were essentially and grossly violated. The Jews to this day maintain, that, whatever were the merits of the case, the trial was at least regular and the sentence legally just; that he was accused of blasphemy, and convicted of that offense by legal evidence. The question between them involves two distinct points of inquiry, namely, first, whether he was guilty of blasphemy and, secondly, whether the arraignment and trial were conducted in the ordinary forms of law. But there will still remain a third question, namely, whether, admitting that, as a mere man, he had violated the law against blasphemy, he could legally be put to death for that cause; and if not, then, whether he was justly condemned upon the new and supplemental accusation of treason or of sedition, which was vehemently urged against him. The first and last of these inquiries it is proposed briefly to pursue; but it will be necessary previously to understand the light in which he was regarded by the Jewish rulers and people, the state of their criminal jurisprudence and course of proceeding, and especially the nature and event of the law concerning blasphemy, upon which he was indicted.

In the early period of the ministry of Jesus, he does not appear to have excited among the Pharisees any emotion but wonder and astonishment, and an intense interest respecting the nature of his mission. But the people heard him with increasing avidity, and followed him in countless throngs. He taught a purer religion than the scribes and Pharisees, whose pride and corruption he boldly denounced. He preached charity and humility, and perfect holiness of heart and life, as essential to the favor of God, whose laws he expounded in all the depth of their spirituality, in opposition to the traditions of the elders, and the false glosses of the scribes and Pharisees. These sects he boldly charged with making void and rejecting the law of God, and enslaving men by their traditions: he accused them of hypocrisy, covetousness, oppression, and lust of power and popularity; and denounced them as hinderers of the salvation of others, as a generation of serpents and vipers, doomed to final perdition. It was natural that these terrific denunciations, from such a personage, supported by his growing power and the increasing acclamations of the people, should alarm the partisans of the ancient theocracy, and lead them to desire his destruction. This alarm evidently increased with the progress of his ministry, and was greatly heightened by the raising of Lazarus from the dead, on which occasion the death of Jesus was definitely resolved on,[1] but no active measures against him seem to have been attempted, until the time when, under the parable of the wicked husbandmen who cast the heir out of the vineyard and killed him, he declared that the kingdom of God should be taken from them, and given to others more worthy. Perceiving that he spoke this parable against them, from that hour they sought to lay hands on him, and were restrained only by fear of the popular indignation.[2]

Having thus determined to destroy Jesus at all events, as a person whose very existence was fatal to their own power, and perhaps, in their view, to the safety of their nation, the first step was to render him odious to the people without which the design would undoubtedly recoil on the heads of its contrivers, his popularity being unbounded. Countless numbers had received the benefit of his miraculous gifts; it was therefore deemed a vain attempt to found an accusation, at that time, on any past transaction of his life. A new occasion was accordingly sought, by endeavoring to "entangle him in his talk," a measure, planned and conducted with consummate cunning and skill. The Jews were divided into two political parties. One of these consisted of the Pharisees, who held it unlawful to acknowledge or pay tribute to the Roman emperor, because they were forbidden, by the law of Moses,[3] to set a king over them who was a stranger, and not one of their own countrymen. The other party was composed of the partisans of Herod, who understood this law to forbid only the voluntary election of a stranger, and therefore esteemed it not unlawful to submit and pay tribute to a conqueror. These two parties, though bitterly opposed to each other, united in the attempt to entrap Jesus, by the question,—"Is it lawful to give tribute to Caesar, or not?"[4] If he answered in the negative, the Herodians were to accuse him to Pilate, for treason; if in the affirmative, the Pharisees would denounce him to the people, as an enemy to their liberties.[5] This insidious design was signally frustrated by the wisdom of his reply, when, referring to Caesar's image and legend, on the coins which they all received as legally current, he showed the inconsistency of withholding the honor due to one thus implicitly acknowledged by both parties to be their lawful sovereign.

Defeated in this attempt to commit him politically, their next endeavor was to render him obnoxious to one or the other of the two great religious sects, which were divided upon the doctrine of the resurrection, the Pharisees affirming and the Sadduces denying, that the dead would rise again. The latter he easily silenced, by a striking exposition of their own law. They asked him which, of several husbands, would be entitled in the next world to the wife whom they successively had married in this; in reply, he showed them that in heaven the relation of husband and wife was unknown.[6]

Their last trial was made by a lawyer, who sought to entrap him into an assertion that one commandment in the law was greater than another; a design rendered abortive by his reply that they were all of equal obligation.[7]

It being apparent, from these successive defeats, that any farther attempt to find new matter of accusation would result only in disgrace to themselves, the enemies of Jesus seem to have come to the determination to secure his person secretly, and afterwards to put him to death, in any manner that would not render them odious to the people. In execution of this design, they first bribed Judas to betray him by night into their hands. This object being attained, the next step was to destroy his reputation, and if possible to render him so vile in the public estimation that his destruction would be regarded with complacency. Now no charge could so surely produce this effect, and none could so plausibly be preferred against him, as that of blasphemy, a crime which the Jews regarded with peculiar horror. Even their veneration of Jesus, and the awe which his presence inspired, had not been sufficient to restrain their rising indignation on several occasions, when they regarded his language as the blasphemous arrogation of a divine character and power to himself; could they now be brought to believe him a blasphemer, and see him legally convicted of this atrocious crime, his destruction might easily be brought about, without any very scrupulous regard to the form, and even with honor to those by whom it might be accomplished.

It will now be necessary to consider more particularly the nature of the crime of blasphemy, in its larger signification, as it may be deduced from the law of God. That the spirit of this law requires from all men, everywhere, and at all times, the profoundest veneration of the Supreme Being, and the most submissive acknowledgment of Him as their rightful sovereign, is too plain to require argument. If proof were wanted, it is abundantly furnished in the Decalogue[8] which is admitted among Christians to be of universal obligation. At the time when the Jewish theocracy was established, idolatry had become generally prevalent, and men had nearly lost all just notions of the nature and attributes of their Creator. It is therefore supposed that the design of Jehovah, in forming the Jewish constitution and code of laws, was to preserve the knowledge of himself as the true God, and to retain that people in the strictest possible allegiance to him alone, totally excluding every acknowledgment of any other being, either as an object of worship or a source of power. Hence the severity with which he required that sorceries, divinations, witchcrafts and false prophecies, as well as open idolatries, should be punished, they being alike acts of treason, or, as we might say, of *praemunire*, amounting to the open acknowledgment of a power independent of Jehovah. Hence, too, the great veneration in which he commanded that his name and attributes should be held, even in ordinary conversation. It is the breach of this last law, to which the term *blasphemy*, in its more restricted sense, has usually been applied[9] but originally the command evidently extended to every word or act,[10] directly in derogation of the sovereignty of Jehovah, such as speaking in the name of another god, or omitting, on any occasion that required it, to give to Jehovah the honor due to his own name.[11] Thus, when Moses and Aaron, at the command of God, struck the rock in Kadesh, that from it waters might flow to refresh the famishing multitude, but neglected to honor him as the source of the miraculous energy, and arrogated it to themselves, saying, "Hear now, ye rebels, must *we* bring you water out of this rock?"[12] this omission drew on them his severe displeasure. "And the Lord spake unto Moses and Aaron, Because ye believed me not, to sanctify *me* in the eyes of the children of Israel, therefore *ye* shall not bring this congregation into the land which I have given them." Accordingly, both Moses and Aaron died before the Israelites entered into the Promised Land.[13] No other deity was permitted to be invoked; no miracle must be wrought, but in the name of God alone. "I am Jehovah; that is my name; and my glory will I not give to another, neither my praise to graven images."[14] This was ever a cardinal principle of his law, neither newly announced by Isaiah, nor by Moses. Its promulgation on Mount Sinai was merely declaratory of what had been well understood at the beginning, namely, that God alone was the Lord of all power and might, and would be expressly acknowledged as such, in every exertion of superhuman energy or wisdom. Thus Joseph, when required to interpret the dream of Pharaoh, replied, "It is not in me: God shall give Pharaoh an answer of peace."[15] And Moses, in all the miracles previously wrought by him in Egypt, expressly denounced them as the judgments of God, by whose hand alone they were inflicted.[16] After the solemn reenactment of this law on Mount Sinai, its signal violation by Moses and Aaron deserved to be made as signal an example of warning; this judgment of Jehovah may be said to constitute the leading case under this article of the law, forming a rule of action and of judgment for all cases of miracles which might be wrought in all coming time. The same principle was afterwards expressly extended to prophesying. "The prophet . . . that shall speak in the name of other gods, even that prophet shall die."[17] His character of prophet, and even his inspiration, shall not authorize him to prophesy but in the name of the Lord. He shall not exercise his office in his own name, nor in any name but that of Jehovah, from whom his power was derived.

That such was understood to be the true meaning of this law of God is further evident from the practice of the prophets, in later times, to whom was given the power of working miracles. These they always wrought in his name, expressly acknowledged at the time. Thus, the miracle of thunder and rain in the season of the wheat harvest, called for by Samuel, he expressly attributed to the Lord.[18] So did Elijah, when he called fire from heaven to consume his sacrifice, in refutation of the claims of Baal.[19] So did Elisha, when he divided the waters of Jordan, by smiting them with the mantle of Elijah;[20] and again, when he miraculously multiplied the loaves of bread for the people that were with him;[21] and again, when he caused the young man's eyes to be opened, that he might behold the hosts of the Lord around him, and smote his enemies with blindness.[22] And even the angel Gabriel, when sent to interpret to Daniel the things which should befall his people in the latter days, explicitly announced himself as speaking in Jehovah's name.[23]

The same view of the sinfulness of exercising superhuman power without an express acknowledgment of God as its author, and of any usurpation of his authority, continued to prevail, down to the time of our Savior. Thus, when he said to the sick of the palsy, "Son, be of good cheer, thy sins be forgiven thee," certain of the scribes said within themselves, "This man blasphemeth. Who can forgive sins, but God alone?"[24] And again, when the Jews, on another occasion, took up stones to stone him, and Jesus, appealing to his good works done among them, asked for which of them he was to be stoned; they replied, "For a good work we stone thee not, but for blasphemy, and because that thou, being a man, makest thyself God."[25] Yet Jesus had on no occasion mentioned the *name* of Jehovah, but with profound reverence.

Thus it appears that the law of blasphemy, as it was understood among the Jews, extended not only to the offense of impiously using the name of the Supreme Being, but to every usurpation of his authority, or arrogation by a created being of the honor and power belonging to him alone.[26] Like the crime of treason among men, its essence consisted in acknowledging or setting up the authority of another sovereign than one's own, or invading the powers pertaining exclusively to him; an offense, of which the case of Moses, before cited, is a prominent instance, both in its circumstances and in its punishment. Whether a false god was acknowledged or the true one denied, and whether the denial was in express terms, or by implication, in assuming to do, by underived power, and in one's own name, that which God only could perform, the offense was essentially the same. And in such horror was it held by the Israelites that in token of it every one was obliged by an early and universal custom to rend his garments, whenever it was committed or related in his presence.[27] This sentiment was deeply felt by the whole people, as a part of their religion.

Such being the general scope and spirit of the law, it would seem to have been easy to prove that Jesus had repeatedly incurred its penalties. He had performed many miracles, but never in any other name than his own. In his own name, and without the recognition of any higher power, he had miraculously healed the sick, restored sight to the blind and strength to the lame, cast out devils, rebuked the winds, calmed the sea, and raised the dead. In his own name, also, and with no allusion to the Omniscient, no "Thus saith the Lord," he had prophesied of things to come. He had by his own authority forgiven sins, and promised, by his own power, not only to raise the dead, but to resume his own life, after he should, as he predicted, be put to death. Finally, he had expressly claimed for himself a divine origin and character, and the power to judge both the living and the dead.[28] Considered as a man, he had usurped the attributes of God. That he was not arrested at an earlier period is to be attributed to his great popularity, and the astounding effect of his miracles. His whole career had been resplendent with beneficence to the thousands who surrounded him. His eloquence surpassed all that had been uttered by man. The people were amazed, bewildered, and fascinated, by the resistless power of his life. It was not until his last triumphal visit to Jerusalem, after he had openly raised Lazarus from the dead, when the chief priests and elders perceived that "the world was gone after him," that they were stricken with dismay and apprehension for their safety, and under this panic resolved upon the perilous measure of his destruction.

The only safe method in which this could be accomplished was under the sanction of a legal trial and sentence. Jesus, therefore, upon his apprehension, was first brought before the great tribunal of the Sanhedrim, and charged with the crime of blasphemy. What were the specifications under this general charge, or whether any were necessary, we are not informed. But that this was the offense charged is manifest both from the evidence adduced and from the judgment of conviction.[29] Such was the estimation in which he was held that it was with great difficulty that witnesses could be found to testify against him; and the two who at last were procured, testified falsely in applying his words to the temple of Solomon which he spoke of the temple of his body. When, upon the occasion of his scourging the money changers out of the temple, the Jews demanded by what authority he did this, Jesus replied, alluding to his own person, "Destroy *this* temple, and in three days I will raise it up.[30] But though the witnesses swore falsely in testifying that he spoke of the Jewish temple, yet his words, in either sense, amounted to a claim of the power of working miracles, and so brought him within the law. The high priest, however, still desirous of new evidence which might justify his condemnation in the eyes of the people, proceeded to interrogate Jesus concerning his character and mission. "I adjure thee, by the living God, that thou tell us whether thou be the Christ, the Son of God. Jesus saith unto him, Thou hast said: nevertheless, I say unto you, hereafter ye shall see the Son of Man sitting on the right hand of power, and coming in the clouds of heaven. Then the high priest *rent his clothes*, saying, He hath *spoken blasphemy*; what *further* need have we of witnesses? Behold, now *ye have heard* his *blasphemy*. What think ye? They answered and said, *He is guilty of death*."[31] We may suppose the multitude standing without the hall of judgment, able, through its avenues and windows, to see, but not to hear, all that was transacting within. It became important, therefore, to obtain some reason upon which the high priest might rend his clothes in their sight, thus giving to the people, by this expressive and awful sign, the highest evidence of blasphemy, uttered by Jesus in the presence of that august assembly. This act turned the tide of popular indignation against him, whose name, but a short time before, had been the theme of their loudest hosannas. There was now no need to go into the past transactions of his ministry for matter of accusation. His friends might claim for him on that score all that the warmest gratitude and love could inspire and all this could be safely conceded. But here, his accusers might say, was a new and shocking crime, just perpetrated in the presence of the most sacred tribunal; a crime so shocking, and so boldly committed, that the high priest rent his clothes with horror, in the very judgment seat, in the presence of all the members of the Sanhedrim, who, with one accord, upon that evidence alone immediately convicted the offender and sentenced him to death.

If we regard Jesus simply as a Jewish citizen, and with no higher character, this conviction seems substantially right in point of law, though the trial was not legal in all its forms. For, whether the accusation was founded on the first or second commands in the Decalogue, or on the law laid down in the thirteenth chapter of Deuteronomy or on that in the eighteenth chapter and twentieth verse, he had violated them all, by assuming to himself powers belonging alone to Jehovah. And even if he were recognized as a prophet of the Lord, he was still obnoxious to punishment, under the decision in the case of Moses and Aaron, before cited. It is not easy to perceive on what ground his conduct could have been defended before any tribunal, unless upon that of his superhuman character. No lawyer, it is conceived, would think of placing his defence upon any other basis.

The great object of exciting the people against Jesus being thus successfully accomplished, the next step was to obtain legal authority to put him to death. For though the Sanhedrim had condemned him, they had not the power to pass a capital sentence, this being a right which had passed from the Jews by the conquest of their country, and now belonged to the Romans alone. They were merely citizens of a Roman province; they were left in the enjoyment of their civil laws, the public exercise of their religion, and many other things relating to their police and municipal regulations; but they had not the power of life and death. This was a principal attribute of sovereignty, which the Romans always took care to reserve to themselves in order to be able to reach those individuals who might become impatient of the yoke, whatever else might be neglected. *Apud quos (Romanos), vis imperii valet; inania transmittuntur.*[32] The jurisdiction of capital cases belonged ordinarily to the governor general or *Praeses* of a province, the *Procurator* having for his principal duty only the charge of the revenue and the cognizance of revenue causes. But the right of taking cognizance of capital crimes was, in some cases, given to certain *Procurators*, who were sent into small provinces, to fill the places of governors, (*Vice Praesides*,) as clearly appears from the Roman laws. The government of all Syria was at this time under a governor general, or *Praeses* of which Judea was one of the lesser dependencies, under the charge of Pilate as *Vice Praeses*, with capital jurisdiction.[33]

It could not be expected that Pilate would trouble himself with the cognizance of any matter not pertaining to the Roman law, much less with an alleged offence against the God of the Jews, who was neither acknowledged nor even respected by their conquerors. Of this the chief priests and elders were fully aware; therefore they prepared a second accusation against Jesus, founded on the Roman law, as likely to succeed with Pilate as the former had done with the people. They charged him with attempting to restore the kingdom of Israel, under his own dominion as king of the Jews. "We found this fellow," said they, "perverting the nation, and forbidding to give tribute to Caesar, saying that he himself is Christ a King."[34]

It was a charge of high treason against the Roman state and emperor, a charge which was clearly within Pilate's cognizance, and which, as they well knew, no officer of Tiberius would venture lightly to regard. Pilate accordingly forthwith arraigned Jesus, and called upon him to answer this accusation. It is worthy of note that from the moment when he was accused of treason before Pilate no further allusion was made to the previous charge of blasphemy, the Roman governor being engaged solely with the charge newly preferred before himself. The answer of Jesus to this charge satisfied Pilate that it was groundless, the kingdom which he set up appearing plainly to be not a kingdom of this world, but his spiritual reign in righteousness and holiness and peace, in the hearts of men. Pilate therefore acquitted him of the offence. "He went out again unto the Jews, and saith unto them, *I find in him no fault at all.*"[35] Here was a sentence of acquittal, judicially pronounced, and irreversible, except by a higher power upon appeal, and it was the duty of Pilate thereupon to have discharged him. But the multitude, headed now by the priests and elders, grew clamorous for his execution adding, "He stirreth up the people, teaching throughout all Jewry, beginning from Galilee to this place."[36] Hearing this reference to Galilee, Pilate seized the opportunity thus offered of escaping from the responsibility of a judgment, either of acquittal or of condemnation, by treating the case as out of his jurisdiction, and within that of Herod, tetrarch of Galilee, who was then in Jerusalem on a visit. He therefore sent Jesus and his accusers to Herod, before whom the charge was vehemently renewed and urged. But Herod, too, perceived that it was utterly groundless, and accordingly treated it with derision, arraying Jesus in mock vestments of royalty, and remanding him to Pilate.[37] The cause was then solemnly re-examined by the Roman governor, and a second judgment of acquittal pronounced. For "Pilate, when he had called together the chief priests and the rulers, and the people, said unto them, Ye have brought this man unto me, as one that perverteth the people; and behold, I having examined him before

you, have found no fault in this man, touching those things whereof
ye accuse him: No, nor yet Herod: for I sent you to him; and lo,
nothing worthy of death is done unto him. I will therefore chastise
him and release him."[38]

It may seem strange to us that after a judgment of acquittal thus
solemnly pronounced, any judge in a civilized country should venture to reverse it, upon the same evidence, and without the pretence
of mistake or error in the proceedings. Probably, in the settled jurisprudence of the city of Rome, it could not have been done. But this
was in a remote province of the empire, under the administration
not of a jurist, but a soldier; and he, too, irresolute and vacillating,
fearful for his office, and even for his life, for be served the "dark and
unrelenting Tiberius." As soon as he proposed to release Jesus, "the
Jews cried out, saying, If thou let this man go, *thou art not Caesar's
friend. Whosoever maketh himself a king speaketh against Caesar.*"[39]
Whereupon "Pilate gave sentence that it should be as they required."[40]
That Jesus was executed under the pretence of treason, and that
alone, is manifest from the tenor of the writing placed over his head,
stating that he was king of the Jews, such being the invariable custom among the Romans, in order that the public might know for
what crime the party had been condemned.[41] The remaining act in
this tragedy is sufficiently known.

In the preceding remarks, the case has been considered only upon
its general merits, and with no reference to the manner in which the
proceedings were conducted. But M. Dupin, in his tract on the
"Trial of Jesus before the Sanhedrim," in reply to Mr. Salvador's
account of it, has satisfactorily shown that throughout the whole
course of that trial the rules of the Jewish law of procedure were
grossly violated, and that the accused was deprived of rights belonging even to the meanest citizen. He was arrested in the night, bound
as a malefactor, beaten before his arraignment, and struck in open
court during the trial; he was tried on a feast day, and before sunrise;
he was compelled to incriminate himself, and this, under an oath of
solemn judicial adjuration; and he was sentenced on the same day of
the conviction. In all these particulars the law was wholly disre-
garded.[42]

Notes

1. See John 11:47–54.
2. Matt. 21:33–46; Mark 22:1–12; Luke 20:9–19.
3. Deut. 17:15.
4. Matt. 22:15–22; Mark 12:13–17; Luke 20:20–26.
5. Tappan's *Jewish Ant.* 239.
6. Matt. 22:23–33; Mark 12:18–27; Luke 20:27–39.
7. Matt. 22:25–40, 46; Mark 12:28–34.
8. Ex. 20:1–7. "And God spake all these words, saying, I *am* the Lord thy God, which have brought thee out of the land of Egypt, out of the house of bondage. Thou shalt have no other gods before me. Thou shalt not make unto thee any graven image, or any likeness of *anything* that *is* in heaven above, or that *is* in the earth beneath, or that *is* in the water under the earth: Thou shalt not bow down thyself to them, nor serve them: for I the Lord thy God *am* a jealous God, visiting the iniquity of the fathers upon the children unto the third and fourth *generation* of them that hate me; And shewing mercy unto thousands of them that love me, and keep my commandments. Thou shalt not take the name of the Lord thy God in vain: for the Lord will not hold him guiltless that taketh his name in vain."
9. Lev. 24:11–16. "And the Israelitish woman's son blasphemed the name *of the Lord*, and cursed; and they brought him unto Moses (and his mother's name *was* Shelomith, the daughter of Dibri, of the tribe of Dan): And they put him in ward, that the mind of the Lord might be shewed them. And the Lord spake unto Moses, saying, Bring forth him that hath cursed without the camp and let all that heard *him* lay their hands upon his head, and let all the congregation stone him. And thou shalt speak unto the children of Israel, saying, Whosoever curseth his God shall bear his sin. And he that blasphemeth the name of the Lord, he shall surely be put to death, *and* all the congregation shall certainly stone him: as well the stranger, as he that is born in the land, when he blasphemeth the name *of the Lord*, shall be put to death." See A. Clarke on Matt. 9:3.
10. Deut. 13:6–10. "If thy brother, the son of thy mother, or thy son, or thy daughter, or the wife of thy bosom, or thy friend, which is as thine own soul, entice thee secretly, saying, Let us go and serve other gods, which thou hast not known, thou, nor thy fathers; *Namely*, of the gods of the people which *are* round about you, nigh unto thee, or far off from thee, from the *one* end of the earth even unto the *other* end of the earth; Thou shalt not consent unto him, nor hearken unto him; neither shall thine eye pity him neither shalt thou spare, neither shalt thou conceal him: But thou shalt surely kill him; thine hand shall be first upon him to put him to death, and afterwards the hand of all the people. And thou shalt stone him with stones that he die; because he had sought to thrust thee away from the Lord thy God, which brought thee

out of the land of Egypt from the house of bondage." Deut. 18:20. "But the prophet, which shall presume to speak a word in my name, which I have not commanded him to speak, or that shall speak in the name of other gods, even that prophet shall die."

11. It is true that in the Mishna it is written—"Blasphemus non tenetur, nisi expressit Nomen." Mishna, Pars 4:242. Tractatus de Syendriis, cap. 7, § 5. But these traditions were not written until 150 years after the time of our Savior; and the passage, moreover, seems properly to refer to that form of blasphemy which consists in evil speaking of the Supreme Being in a direct manner, rather than to the other forms in which this offense, in its larger acceptation, might be committed. See Michaelis Comm. Art. 251. Vol. 4, pp. 67–70.

12. Num. 20:10, 12.

13. Num. 20:24; Deut. 1:37; 34:4–5.

14. Is. 42:8; 48:2.

15. Gen. 41:16, 25, 28.

16. Ex. 8–10 per tot.

17. Deut. 18:20.

18. "Now, therefore, stand and see this great thing, which the Lord will do before your eyes" (1 Sam. 12:16–18).

19. "And it came to pass, at the time of the offering of the evening sacrifice, that Elijah the prophet came near and said, Lord God of Abraham, Isaac, and of Israel, let it be known this day that *thou art God in Israel,*" &c. 1 Kings 18:36–38.

20. "And he took the mantle of Elijah that fell from him, and smote the waters, and said, *Where is the Lord God of Elijah?*" (2 Kings 2:14).

21. "*For thus saith the Lord*, they shall eat and shall leave thereof " (2 Kings 4:43).

22. See 2 Kings 6:16–20. In some other places, where there is no express reference to the power of God, the omission may be attributed to the brevity of the narrative; but even in those cases, such reference is plainly implied.

23. Dan. 9:21, 23; 10:12. See further, 2 Kings 18:30–35; 19:1–3.

24. Matt. 9:2–3; Luke 5:20–21.

25. John 10:31–33.

26. This view of the Jewish law may seem opposed to that of Dr. Campbell, in his Preliminary Dissertations on the Gospels, (Vol. 2 Diss. 9 Part 2); but it is evident, on examination, that he is discussing the *word blasphemy,* and the propriety of its application, taken in its more restricted sense of intentional and direct malediction of Jehovah, and not whether the assumption of his attributes and authority was or was not a violation of his law. That this assumption was a heinous transgression seems universally agreed. The question, therefore, is reduced to this—whether the offense was properly *termed*

blasphemy. For the *act*, by whatever name it was called, was a capital crime. The Jewish judges of that day held it to amount to blasphemy, and in so doing they do not appear to have given to their law a construction more expanded and comprehensive than has been given by judges in our own times to the law of treason or of sedition.

27. This was judicially and solemnly done by the members of the Sanhedrim, rising from their seats, when the crime was testified to. Only one witness was permitted to repeat the words; the others simply stating that they heard the same which he had related. The practice is thus described in the Mishna: "Exactis omnibus, interrogant vetustissimum testium, dicendo,—*Edissere, quodcumque audivisti expresse.* Tum ille hoc refert. Judices autem stant erecti, vestesque discerpunt, non resarciendas. Dein secundus tertiusque ait, —*Ego idem, quod ille, audivi.*" Mishna, Pars 4, *Tractat de Synedriss*, cap 7, § 8. Upon which Cocceius remarks,—"Assurgunt reverentiae causa. Mos discendarum vestium probatur ex 2do Regum, 18:37. Hinc nata est regula,— *Qui blasphemiamaudit, vel ab ipso auctore vel ex alio, tenetur vestem discerpere.* Ratio est, ut semper ob oculos et animum versetur maeroris aut indignationis mnemosynon." Coccej. in loc, § 11–12. The custom is fully explained, with particular reference to the high priest at the trial of Jesus by Hedenus, *De Scissione Vestium* 38, 42, (In *Ugolini Thesauro*, tom. 29 fol. 1025)

28. That the Jews understood Jesus to make himself equal with God is maintained by Mr. Salvadore, himself a Jew, in his *Histoire des Institutions de Moise et du Peuple Hebreu*, Liv. 4:3, p. 81, of which chapter a translation is given at the end of this article. Mr. Noah, also a Jew, seems to be of opinion that Jesus was brought to trial under the law in Deut. 13:1–11. See his "Discourse on the Restoration of the Jews," p. 19. But whether he was charged with a blasphemous usurpation of the attributes of deity, or with sedition, in inciting the people to serve another god, meaning himself, the difference is of no importance, the essence of the offense in both cases being the same.

29. Matt. 26:59–65. This view of the nature of the offense with which Jesus was charged is confirmed by the learned jurist, Chr. Thomasius, in his "Dissertatio de injusto Pilati judicio," § 11–12, and by the authors whom he there cites. *Dissert. Thomasii.* vol. 1, p. 5.

30. John 2:13–22.

31. Matt. 26:63–66.

32. Tacit. *Annal.* 15:31. See M. Dupin's *Trial of Jesus*, pp. 57–59, (Amer. Ed.) Chr. Thomasius, "Dissertatio de injusto Pilati judicio," § 12, 60. The want of this power was admitted by the Jews in their reply to Pilate, when he required them to judge Jesus according to their own law, and they replied, "It is not lawful for us to put any man to death." John 18:31.

This point has been held in different ways by learned men. Some are of opinion that the Sanhedrim had power to inflict death for offenses touching religion, though not for political offences, and that it was with reference to the charge of treason that they said to Pilate what has just been cited from St. John. They say that, though the Sanhedrim had convicted Jesus of blasphemy, yet they dared not execute that sentence, for fear of a sedition of the people—that they therefore craftily determined to throw on Pilate the odium of his destruction, by accusing him of treason; hence, after condemning him, they consulted further, as stated in Matt. 27:1–2; Mark 15:1, how to effect this design—that when Pilate found no fault in him, and directed them to take and crucify him, some replied, "We have a law, and by our law he ought to die," (John 19:7) to intimate to Pilate that Jesus was guilty of death by the Jewish law also, as well as the Roman, and that therefore he would not lose any popularity by condemning him. See Zorrius, *His. Fisci Judaici*, ch. 2, § 2, (in *Ugolini Thesauro* tom. 26, col. 1001–1003.) The same view is taken by Deylingius, *De Judoeorum Jure Gladii*, § 10–12, (in *Ugolini Thesauro* tom. 29, col. 1189–1192.) But he concludes that in all capital cases there was an appeal from the Sanhedrim to the Praetor, and that without the approval of the latter, the sentence of the Sanhedrim could not be executed. Ibid. § 15, col. 1196. Molinaeus understood the Jewish law in the same manner. See his *Harmony of the Gospels*, note on John 18:31. C. Molinaei Opera, tom. 5, pp. 603–604. But this opinion is refuted by what is said by M. Dupin, *Trial* § 8, and by Thomasius.

33. See M. Dupin, *Trial of Jesus*, pp. 55–62. His authorties are Loiseau-Godefroy, and Cujas, the two latter of whom he cites as follows: "Procurator Caesaris *fungens vice praesidis* potest cognoscere *de causis criminalibus*. Godefroy, in his note (letter S) upon the 3rd law of the code, *Ubi causae fiscales*. And he cites several others, which I have verified, and which are most precise to the same effect. See particularly the 4th law of the Code, *Ad. leg. fab. de plag.*, and the 2nd law of the Code, *De Poenis.*—Procuratoribus Caesaris data est jurisdictio in causis fiscalibus pecuniarniis. non in criminalibus, nisi quum fungebantur *vice praesidum;* ut Pontius Pilatus fuit procurator Caesaris *vics praesidis* in Syria. Cujas, *Observ.* 19:13."

34. Luke 23:2.

35. John 18:38.

36. Luke 23:5.

37. Luke 23:10–11.

38. Luke 23:13–15. I regard this judgment as conclusive evidence of the innocence of the accused. Pilate's strenuous endeavours to release him instead of Barabbas, and his solemn washing his own hands of the guilt of his

blood, though they show the strength of his own convictions, yet add no legal force to the judgment itself.

39. John 19:12.
40. Luke 23:24.
41. See M. Dupin's *Trial of Jesus*, pp. 82–84.
42. Ibid., pp. 7–15; *John's Bibl. Ant.* § 246.

The Jewish Account of the Trial of Jesus

by Joseph Salvador

Introduction by Mr. Greenleaf

Mr. Joseph Salvador, a physician and a learned Jew, a few years ago published at Paris a work entitled *Histoire des Institutions de Moise et due Peuple Hebreu,* in which, among other things, he gives an account of their course of criminal procedure in a chapter on "The Administration of Justice"; which he illustrates in a succeeding chapter by an account of the trial of Jesus. As this is the recent work of a man of learning, himself a Jew, it may be regarded as an authentic statement of what is understood and held by the most intelligent and best informed Jews respecting the claims of our Lord, the tenor of his doctrines, the nature of the charge laid against him before the Sanhedrim, and the grounds on which they condemned him. The following translation of the last-mentioned chapter will therefore not be unacceptable to the reader. It will be found in Book 4, chapter 3, entitled, "The Trial and Condemnation of Jesus." The reader will bear in his mind that it is the language of an enemy of our Savior, and in justification of his murderers.

Preface by Mr. Salvadore

According to this exposition of judicial proceedings, I shall follow out the application of them in the most memorable trial in history, that of Jesus Christ. I have already explained the motives which have directed me and the point of view in which I have considered the subject; I have already shown, that among the Jews no title was a shelter against a prosecution and sentence. Whether the law or its forms were good or bad, is not the object of my present investigation; neither is it to ascertain whether we ought to pity the blindness of the Hebrews in not discovering a Deity in Jesus, or to be astonished that a God personified could not make himself comprehended when he desired it. But since they regarded him only as a citizen, did they not try him according to their law and its existing forms? This is my question, which can admit of no equivocation. I shall draw all my facts from the Evangelists themselves, without inquiring whether all this history was developed after the event, to serve as a form to a new doctrine, or to an old one which had received a fresh impulse.

Jesus was born of a family of small fortune; Joseph, his supposed father, perceived that his wife was big before they had come together. If he had brought her to trial, in the ordinary course of things, Mary, according to the verse 23 chapter 22 of Deuteronomy, would have been condemned, and Jesus, having been declared illegitimate, could never, according to verse 2 chapter 23, have been admitted to a seat in the Sanhedrim.[1] But Joseph, who, to save his wife from disgrace, had taken the resolution of sending her away privately, soon had a dream which consoled him.[2]

After having been circumcised, Jesus grew like other men, attended the solemn feasts, and early displayed surprising wisdom and sagacity. In the assembly on the Sabbath, the Jews eager for the disputes to which the interpretation of the law gave rise, loved to hear him. But he soon devoted himself to more important labors; he pronounced censures against whole towns, Capernaum, Chorazin and Bethsaida.[3] Recalling the times of Isaiah and Jeremiah, he thundered against the chiefs of the people with a vehemence which would in our day be terrific.[4] The people then regarded him as a prophet;[5] they heard him preach in towns and country without opposition; they saw him surrounded with disciples according to the custom of the learned men of the age; whatever may have been the resentment of the chief men, they were silent as long as he confined himself to the law.

But Jesus, in presenting new theories, and in giving new forms to those already promulgated, speaks of himself as God; his disciples repeat it; and the subsequent events prove in the most satisfactory manner, that they thus understood him.[6] This was shocking blasphemy in the eyes of the citizens: the law commands them to follow Jehovah alone, the only true God; not to believe in gods of flesh and bone, resembling men or women; neither to spare nor listen to a prophet who, even doing miracles, should proclaim a new god, a god neither they nor their fathers had known.[7]

Jesus having said to them one day: "I have come down from heaven to do these things," the Jews, who till then had listened to him, murmured and cried: "Is not this Jesus, the son of Joseph and of Mary? we know his father, his mother, and his brethren; why then does he say that he has come down from heaven ?"[8] On another day, the Jews, irritated from the same cause, took stones and threatened him. Jesus said unto them, "I have done good works in your eyes by the power of my Father, for which of these works would you stone me?" "It is for no good work," replied the Jews, who stated the whole process in few words, "but because of thy blasphemy; for being a man,[9] thou makest thyself God."[10]

His language was not always clear. Often his disciples themselves did not comprehend him. Among his maxims, some of which showed the greatest mildness, there were some which the Hebrews, who were touched only through their natural sense, thought criminal. "Think not that I am come to send peace on earth; I came not to send peace, but a sword. For I am come to set a man at variance against his father, and the daughter against her mother, and the daughter-in-law against her mother-in-law. And a man's foes shall be they of his own household. He that loveth father or mother more than me, is not worthy of me."[11] Finally, if he wrought miracles before certain of the people, his replies to the questions of the doctors were generally evasive.[12]

In regard to political relations, he caused dissensions.[13] A great number of disorderly persons whom he had the design of reclaiming, but who inspired dread in the national council, attached themselves to him,[14] his discourse flattered them inasmuch as he pronounced anathemas against riches. "Know," said he, "that it is easier for a camel to go through the eye of a needle, than for a rich man to enter the kingdom of heaven."[15] In this state of affairs, the council deliberates; some are of opinion that he should be regarded as a madman,[16] others say that he seeks to seduce the people.[17] Caiaphas, the high priest, whose dignity compels him, to defend the letter of the law, observes that these dissensions would furnish an excuse to the Romans for overwhelming Judea, and that the interests of the whole nation must outweigh those of a single individual; he constitutes himself the accuser of Jesus.[18]

The order is given to seize him. But let us pause here upon a fact of the highest importance. The senate did not begin by actually seizing Jesus, as is now the practice they begin by giving, after some debate, an order that he should be seized.[19] This decree is made public; it is known to all, especially to Jesus. No opposition is offered to his passing the frontier: his liberty depends entirely upon himself. This is not all; the order for his arrest was preceded by a decree of admonition. One day, Jesus having entered the temple, took upon himself authority contrary to the common law; then he preached to the people, and said: "That those who should believe in him should be able to do all things, so that if they should say to a mountain, remove thyself and cast thyself into the sea, it would obey." Then the chief priest and senators went to find him and said to him, "By what authority doest thou things? who gave thee this power?"[20]

Meanwhile a traitor discloses the place whither the accused had retired; the guards, authorized by the high priest and by the elders,[21] hasten to seize him. One of his disciples, breaking into open rebellion, with a stroke of his sword cuts off the ear of one of them, and brings upon himself the reproof of his master.[22] As soon as Jesus is arrested, the zeal of his apostles is extinguished; all forsake him.[23] He is brought before the grand council, where the priests sustain the accusation. The witnesses testify, and they are numerous; for the deeds of which he is accused were done in the presence of all the people. The two witnesses whom St. Matthew and St. Mark accuse of perjury, relate a discourse which St. John declares to be true, with regard to the power which Jesus arrogates to himself.[24] Finally, the high priest addresses the accused, and says: "Is it true that thou art Christ, that thou art the Son of God?" "I am he." replies Jesus; "you shall see me hereafter at the right hand of the majesty of God, who shall come upon the clouds of heaven." At these words, Caiaphas rent his garments in token of horror.[25] "You have heard him." They deliberate. The question already raised among the people was this: Has Jesus become God? But the senate having adjudged that Jesus, son of Joseph, born at Bethlehem, had profaned the name of God by usurping it to himself, a mere citizen, applied to him the law of blasphemy, and the law in the 13th chapter of Deuteronomy, and the 20th verse in chapter 18, according to which every prophet, even he who works miracles, must be punished, when he speaks of a god unknown to the Jews and their fathers:[26] the capital sentence was pronounced. As to the ill-treatment which followed the sentence, it was contrary to the spirit of the Jewish law and it is not in the course of nature, that a senate composed of the most respectable men of a nation, who, however, they might have been deceived, yet intended to act legally, should have permitted such outrages against him whose life was at their disposal. The writers who have transmitted to us these details, not having been present at the trial, have been disposed to exaggerate the picture, either on account of their prejudices, or to throw greater contempt on the judges.

One thing is certain, that the council met again on the morning of the next day or the day following that,[27] as the law requires, to confirm or to annul the sentence: it was confirmed. Jesus was brought before Pilate, the procurator that the Romans had placed over the Jews. They had retained the power of trying according to their own laws, but the executive power was in the hands of the procurator alone: no criminal could be executed without his consent: this was in order that the Senate should not have the means of reaching men who were sold to foreigners.[28] Pilate, the Roman, signed the decree. His soldiers, an impure mixture of diverse nations, were charged with the punishment. These are they who brought Jesus to the judgment hall, who stripped him before the whole cohort, who placed upon his head a crown of thorns, and a reed in his hand, who showed all the barbarity to which the populace in all ages is disposed; who finally caused him to undergo a punishment common at Rome, and which was not in use among the Jews.[29] But before the execution, the governor had granted to the condemned an appeal to the people, who, respecting the judgment of their own council, would not permit this favor, couching their refusal in these terms: "We have a law; and by our law he ought to die, because he made himself the Son of God."[30] Then Pilate left them the choice of saving Jesus, or a man accused of murder in a sedition; the people declared for the latter; saying that the other would scatter the seeds of discord in the bosom of the nation, at a time when union was most necessary.[31]

Jesus was put to death. The priests and elders went to the place of punishment; and as the sentence was founded upon this fact, that he had unlawfully arrogated to himself the title of Son of God, God himself, they appealed to him thus: "Thou wouldst save others; thyself thou canst not save. If thou art indeed the king of Israel, come down into the midst of us, and we will believe in thee; since thou hast said, I am the Son of God, let that God who loves thee come now to thine aid.[32] According to the Evangelist, these words were a mockery; but the character of the persons who pronounced them, their dignity, their age, the order which they had observed in the trial, prove their good faith. Would not a miracle at this time have been decisive?"

Notes
1. Deut. 22:22; 23:2. Selden De Synedriis, lib. 3 cap. 4–5.
2. Matt. 1:19–20.
3. Matt. 11:20–24; Luke 4.
4. Matt. 23.
5. Matt. 21:11–46; John 7:40.

6. The expression *son of God* was in common use among the Jews, to designate a man of remarkable wisdom and piety. It was not in this sense that Jesus Christ used it; for in that case it would have occasioned no great sensation. Besides, If we should assume, in order to make it a subject of accusation against these Jew's, that Jesus did not expressly declare himself to be God, we should be exposed to this rejoinder: Why then do you believe in him?

7. See Deut. 4:15 and Deut. 13.

8. John 11:39–42; Matt. 13:55.

9. This fact is as clearly established as possible; and we must observe that till then there had been neither opposition nor enmity in the minds of this people, since they had listened to him with the greatest attention, and did not hesitate to acknowledge in him all that the public law permitted them to do, namely, a prophet, a highly inspired man.

10. John 10:30–33.

11. Matt. 10:34; Mark 10:29.

12. Matt. 16:1–4; John 8:13–18.

13. John 7:43; Luke 23:5.

14. Matt. 9:10; Mark 2:15; Luke 15:1.

15. Matt. 19:24.

16. John 10:20.

17. John 7:12.

18. John 11:47–50.

19. Matt. 26:4; John 11:53–54.

20. Matt. 21:23.

21. It will be recollected, that the senate held its sessions in one of the porticos of the temple. At this time the high priest presided over the senate, so that the guards of the high priest, of the elders and the temple, were no other than the legal militia.

22. John 18:10–11.

23. Mark 14:50; Matt. 26:56.

24. Matt. 26:60–61. And the last came two false witnesses, and said, This fellow said, I am able to destroy the temple of God, and to build it in three days. Mark 14:57–58. And there arose certain and bare false witness against him, saying, We heard him say, I will destroy this temple that is made with hands, and within three days I will build another made without hands. John 2:19–22. Jesus answered and said unto them, Destroy this temple, and in three days I will raise it up. But he spake of the temple of his body. When, therefore, he was risen from the dead, his disciples remembered that he said this unto them; and they believed the Scripture, and the word which Jesus had said.

25. I repeat that the expression *son of God*, includes here the idea of God

himself; the fact is already established, and all the subsequent events confirm it. Observe, also, that I quote the narrative of only one of the parties to this great proceeding.

26. Deut. 28:20. But the prophet, which shall presume to speak a word in my name, which I have not commanded him to speak, or that shall speak in the name of other gods, even that prophet shall die.

27. Matt. 27:1; Mark 15:1.

28. The duties of Pilate were to inform himself whether the sentences given did or did not affect the interests of Rome; there his part ended. Thus it is not astonishing that this procurator, doubtless little acquainted with the Jewish laws, signed the decree for the arrest of Jesus, although he did not find him guilty. We shall see hereafter that there were then many parties among the Jews, among whom were the Herodians or serviles, partisans of the house of Herod, and devoted to the foreign interests. These are they who speak continually of Caesar, of rendering to Caesar the tribute due to Caesar; they also insist that Jesus called himself *king of the Jews:* but this charge was reckoned as nothing before the senate, and was not of a nature alone to merit capital punishment.

29. See Matt. 27:27; Mark 15:16; John 19:2.

30. John 19:7.

31. The sending back of Jesus to Herod, which, according to the Gospel of St. Luke, Pilate would have done, is not stated by the other Evangelists, and does not at all change the judicial question. Herod Antipas, tetrarch of Galilee, and of Perea, had no authority in Jerusalem. Upon his visit to this city, Pilate, according to St. Luke, would, out of respect, have caused Jesus to appear before this ally of the Romans, because Jesus was surnamed the Galilean, though originally from Judea. But to whatever tribe he belonged, the nature of the accusation would still have required, according to the Hebrew law, that he should be judged by the senate of Jerusalem.

32. Matt. 17:42–43.

The Trial of Jesus Before Caiaphas and Pilate

A refutation of Mr. Salvador's chapter entitled
"The Trial and Condemnation of Jesus"
(Included in this volume as
"The Jewish Account of the Trial of Jesus")

by M. Dupin
Advocate and Doctor of Laws

If thou let this man go, thou art not Ceasar's friend.

—John 19:12

Translated from the French
by John Pickering, LL.D.,
Counselor-at-law, and president of the
American Academy of Arts and Sciences.

Preface

A few years ago, Mr. Joseph Salvador, a physician—and a descendant of one of those Jewish families whom the intolerance of Ferdinand the Catholic expelled, in a body, from Spain about the year 1482—published at Paris a lead work, entitled *Histoire des Institutions de Moise et du Peuple Hebreu,* or *History of the Institutions of Moses and the Hebrew People;* and in one chapter of his work he gives an account of the "Administration of Justice" among the Hebrews. To that chapter he has subjoined an account of the "Trial and Condemnation of Jesus" [included in this volume as "The Jewish Account of the Trial of Jesus."] in the course of which he expresses his opinion that the trial, considered merely as a legal proceeding, was conformable to the Jewish laws.

The author of the following little work, M. Dupin, who is one of the most eminent lawyers of French Bar, immediately called in question the correctness of Mr. Salvador's opinion, and entered upon an analysis of this portion of his work, with a view to examine its soundness; the present volume contains the result of that examination, conducted with great legal skill and extensive learning.

It appears that he had many years before, in a little work entitled *The Free Defense of Accused Persons,* published in 1815, taken the same views of this great trial; which, as he observes, has been justly called "the Passion or Suffering of our Savior; for he did in truth suffer, and had not a trial."

The author's attention, however, had been withdrawn from this subject for several years, when it was again brought under his notice by the work of Mr. Salvador, a copy of which was sent to him by that writer, with a request that M. Dupin would give some account of it. Accordingly, says the latter, "it is in compliance with his request, and not from a spirit of hostility, that I have made this examination of his work," and he gives ample proof of his good feeling towards Mr. Salvador, with whom, he says, he is personally acquainted and for whose talents he has a great respect.

With this friendly spirit he enters upon his examination which is conducted with an ability, learning, animation, and interest that leave nothing to be desired. As an argument, his work is unanswerable—he has demolished that of his adversary; and, for intense interest, we do not know any publication of the present day to be compared with it.

The introductory analysis of Mr. Salvador's chapter on the "Administration of Justice according to the Jewish Law" will be highly instructive and interesting, and those persons who have not been accustomed to read the Bible with particular reference to the Law, will find many new and striking views of that portion of the Scriptures. They cannot fail to be particularly struck with the extraordinary care taken to secure by law the personal liberty and rights of the citizen.

According to Mr. Salvador's view, "the fundamental division into castes is the principal basis of the oriental theocracies." Moses, on the contrary, took for his basis the unity of the people. In his system of legislation the people are everything; and the author shows us that every thing, eventually, is done for them, by them, and with them. The tribe of Levi was established only to supply a secondary want; and that tribe was very far from obtaining all the powers which we are apt to attribute to it; it did not make, nor develop the laws; it does not judge or govern; all its members, even the high priest himself, were subject to the control of the Elders of the nation, or of a Senate legally assembled.

Intimately connected with these rights of the people was the liberty of speech; Mr. Salvador, in his chapter on the "Public Orators and Prophets," maintains, and in the opinion of Dupin, proves clearly, that in no nation was the liberty of speech ever so unlimited, as among the Hebrews. Accordingly he observes—"What an additional difference was this between the Israelites and the Egyptians! Among the latter, the mass of the people did not dare without incurring the hazard of the most terrible punishment, to utter a word on affairs of state; it was Harpocrates, the god of silence with his finger on his closed lips, who was their God; in Israel, it was the right of speech."

But we forbear any further reflections, and submit this remarkable performance to our readers. Those who are familiar with the animated tone of French writers will perhaps discover in this translation some loss of the fire and intensity of the original; but the translator's purpose will be effected, if his version shall be found to be a faithful one.

September 3, 1839

Introduction

Analysis of the Chapter of Mr. Salvador Entitled "The Administration of Justice Among the Jews."

Mr. Salvador has discussed with particular care whatever relates to the *administration of justice*[1] among the Jewish people. We shall dwell upon this chapter, which undoubtedly will most interest our readers.

Judicare and *judicari*, to judge and to be judged, express the rights of every Hebrew citizen; that is, no one could be condemned without a judgment, and every one might, in his turn, be called upon to sit in judgment upon others. Some exceptions to this principle are explained but they do not affect the rule. In matters of mere interest each party chose a judge, and these two chose a third person. If a discussion arose as to *the interpretation of a law*, they carried it to the lower council of Elders, and from thence to the Great Council at Jerusalem. Each town of more than one hundred and twenty families was to have its lower council, consisting of twenty-three members; these had jurisdiction in criminal cases.

The expressions, *he shall die, he shall be cut off from the people*, which are so often used in the Mosaic law, embrace three very different significations, which we are accustomed to confound. They indicate the suffering of death as a punishment, civil death, and that premature death with which an individual is naturally threatened who departs from those rules which are useful to the nation and to the individual himself. Civil death is the last degree of *separation*, or *excommunication*; it is pronounced, as a judicial punishment, by the assembly of the judges.

There were three kinds of separation, which Mr. Salvador compares to the three degrees of civil excommunication provided for in the French Penal Code, and which condemn the criminal to hard labor either for life or for a term of years, or to certain correctional punishments. But the Hebrew excommunication had this advantage, that the party *never lost all hope of regaining his original standing*.

The Hebrew lawyers, in relation to the punishment of death, maintained opinions which deserve to be quoted:

A tribunal, which condemns to death *once in seven years,* may be called *sanguinary*—"It deserves this appellation," says Doctor Eliezer, "when it pronounces a like sentence once in seventy years."—"If we had been members of the high court," say the doctors Tyrphon and Akiba, "we should never have condemned a man to death." Simeon, the son of Gamaliel, replied—"Would not that be an abuse? Would you not have been afraid of multiplying crimes in Israel?" Mr. Salvador answers—"No, certainly; far from lessening their number, the severity of the punishment increases it, by giving a more resolute character to the men who are able to brave it; and, at the present day, how many intelligent minds range themselves on the side of Akiba and Tyrphon! How many consciences refuse to participate, in any manner, in the death of a man! The flowing of blood, the multitude excited by an unbecoming curiosity, the victim dragged in triumph to the horrible altar, the impossibility of repairing a mistake, (from which human wisdom is never exempt), the dread of one day seeing a departed shade rising up and saying, '*I was innocent,*' the facility which modern nations have of expelling from among them the man whose presence pollutes them—the influence of general depravity on the production of crimes—and finally the absurd contrast of the whole of society, while in possession of strength, intelligence, and arms, opposing itself to an individual wretch (who has been drawn on by want, by passion, or by ignorance) and yet finding no other means of redress than by exceeding him in cruelty—all these things, and many others, have so deeply penetrated the minds of all ranks of people, that there will one day proceed from them the most striking proof of the power of morals over the laws; for the law will be changed by the simple fact, that we shall not find any person who will consent to apply it.

I feel honored in having maintained the same opinion in my *Observations on Criminal Legislation;* but I solicit those who wish to see this question discussed in its whole extent, to read the profound reflections which the Duke de Broglie has just published on the subject, in the last number of the *Revue Francaise* (for October, 1828).

The whole criminal procedure in the Pentateuch rests upon three principles, which may be thus expressed: publicity of the trial, entire liberty of defense allowed to the accused, and a guaranty against the dangers of testimony. According to the Hebrew text *one* witness is no witness; there must be at least two or three who know the fact. The witness who testifies against a man, must swear that he speaks the truth; the judges then proceed to take exact information of the matter; and, if it is found that the witness has sworn falsely, they compel him to undergo the punishment to which he would have exposed his neighbor. The discussion between the accuser and the accused is conducted before the whole assembly of the people. When a man is condemned to death, those witnesses whose evidence decided the sentence inflict the first blows, in order to add the last degree of certainty to their evidence. Hence the expression—*Let him among you who is without sin, cast the first stone.*

If we pursue their application of these fundamental rules in practice, we shall find that a trial proceeded in the following manner.

On the day of the trial, the executive officers of justice caused the accused person to make his appearance. At the feet of the Elders were placed men who, under the name of *auditors*, or *candidates*, followed regularly the sittings of the Council. The papers in the case were read, and the witnesses were called in succession. The president addressed this exhortation to each of them: "It is not conjectures, or whatever public rumor has brought to thee, that we ask of thee; consider that a great responsibility rests upon thee: that we are not occupied by an affair, like a case of pecuniary interest, in which the injury may be repaired. If thou causest the condemnation of a person unjustly accused, his blood, and the blood of all the posterity of him, of whom thou wilt have deprived the earth, will fall upon thee; God will demand of thee an account, as he demanded of Cain an account of the blood of Abel. Speak."

A woman could not be a witness, because she would not have the courage to give the first blow to the condemned person; nor could a child, that is irresponsible, nor a slave, nor a man of bad character, nor one whose infirmities prevent the full enjoyment of his physical and moral faculties. *The simple confession of an individual against himself,* or the declaration of a prophet, however renowned, would not decide a condemnation. The Doctors say, "We hold it as fundamental, that *no one shall prejudice himself.* If a man accuses himself before a tribunal, we must not believe him, unless the fact is attested by two other witnesses; and it is proper to remark, that the punishment of death inflicted upon Achan, in the time of Joshua[2] was an exception, occasioned by the nature of the circumstances; for our law does not condemn upon the simple confession of the accused, nor upon the declaration of one prophet alone."

The witnesses were to attest to the identity of the party, and to depose to the month, day, hour, and circumstances of the crime. After an examination of the proofs, those judges who believed the party innocent stated their reasons; those who believed him guilty spoke afterwards, and *with the greatest moderation.* If one of the *auditors,* or *candidates,* was entrusted by the accused with his defense, or if he wished in his own name to present any elucidations in favor of innocence, he was admitted to the seat, from which he addressed the judges and the people. But this liberty was not granted to him, if his opinion was in favor of condemning. Lastly when the accused person himself wished to speak, they gave the most profound attention. When the discussion was finished, one of the judges recapitulated the case; they removed all the spectators; two scribes took down the votes of the judges; one of them noted those who were in favor of the accused, and the other, those who condemned him. Eleven votes, out of twenty-three, were sufficient to acquit; but it required thirteen to convict. If any of the judges stated that they were not sufficiently informed, there were added two more Elders, and then two others in succession, till they formed a council of sixty-two, which was the number of the Grand Council. If a majority of votes acquitted, the accused was discharged *instantly;* if he was to be punished, the judges postponed pronouncing sentence till the third day; during the intermediate day they could not be occupied with anything but the cause, and they abstained from eating freely, and from wine, liquors, and everything which might render their minds less capable of reflection.

On the morning of the third day they returned to the judgment seat. Each judge who had not changed his opinion said, *I continue of the same opinion and condemn;* any one who at first condemned, might at this sitting acquit; but he who at once acquitted was not allowed to condemn. If a majority condemned, two *magistrates* immediately accompanied the condemned person to the place of punishment. The Elders did not descend from their seats; they placed at the entrance of the judgment hall an officer of justice with a small flag in his hand; a second officer, on horseback, followed the prisoner, and constantly kept looking back to the place of departure. During this interval, if any person came to announce to the elders any new evidence favorable to the prisoner, the first officer waved his flag, and the second one, as soon as he perceived it, brought back the prisoner. If the prisoner declared to the *magistrates* that he recollected some reasons which had escaped him, they brought him before the *judges* no less than five times. If no incident occurred, the procession advanced slowly, preceded by a herald who, in a loud voice, addressed the people thus: "This man (stating his name and surname) is led to punishment for such a crime; the witnesses who have sworn against him are such and such persons; if any one has evidence to give in his favor, let him come forth quickly."

It was in consequence of this rule that the youthful Daniel caused the procession to go back, which was leading Susanna to punishment, and he himself ascended the seat of justice to put some new questions to the witnesses.

At some distance from the place of punishment, they urged the prisoner to confess his crime, and they made him drink a stupefying beverage, in order to render the approach of death less terrible.[3]

By this mere analysis of a part of Mr. Salvador's work we may judge of the extreme interest of the whole. His principal object has been to make apparent the mutual aids which history, philosophy, and legislation afford in explaining the institutions of the Jewish people. His book is a scientific work, and at the same time a work of taste. His notes indicate vast reading; in the choice of his citations he gives proofs of his critical skill and discrimination. Mr. Salvador belongs, by his age, to that new generation which is distinguished as much by its application to solid studies, as by elevation and generosity of sentiment.

The Trial of Jesus

Refutation of the chapter of Mr. Salvador, entitled "The Trial and Condemnation of Jesus"

The chapter in which Mr. Salvador treats of the "Administration of Justice among the Hebrews," is altogether theoretical. He makes an exposition of *the law*—that things, in order to be *conformable to rule*, must be transacted in a certain mode. In all this I have not contradicted him, but have let him speak for himself.

In the subsequent chapter the author announces: "That according to this *exposition of judicial proceedings* he is going to follow out the application of them to the most memorable trial in all history, that of Jesus Christ." Accordingly the chapter is entitled: "The Trial and Condemnation of Jesus. [Included in this volume as "The Jewish Account of the Trial of Jesus."].

The author first takes care to inform us under what point of view he intends to give an account of that accusation: "That we ought to lament the blindness of the Hebrews for not having recognized a God in Jesus, is a point which I do not examine." (There is another thing also, which he says he shall not examine.) "But, when they discovered in him *only a citizen*, did they try him *according to existing laws and formalities?*"

The question being thus stated, Mr. Salvador goes over all the various aspects of the accusation; and his conclusion is, that the procedure was perfectly regular, and the condemnation perfectly appropriate to the act committed. "Now," says he, "the Senate, having adjudged that Jesus, the son of Joseph, born in Bethlehem, had profaned the name of God by usurping it himself, though a simple citizen, applied to him the law against blasphemy, the law in the 13th chapter of Deuteronomy, and chapter 18, verse 20, according to which every prophet, even one that performs miracles, is to be punished when he speaks of a God unknown to the Hebrews or their fathers."

This conclusion is formed to please the followers of the Jewish law; it is wholly for their benefit, and the evident object is, to justify them from the reproach of *deicide*.

We will, however avoid treating this grave subject in a theological

point of view. As to myself, Jesus Christ is the *Man-God;* but it is not
with arguments drawn from my religion and my creed, that I intend
to combat the statement and the conclusion of Mr. Salvador. The
present age would charge me with being intolerant and this is a
reproach which I will never incur. Besides, I do not wish to give to
the enemies of Christianity the advantage of making the outcry, that
we are afraid to enter into a discussion with them, and that we wish
to crush rather than to convince them. Having thus contented myself with declaring my own faith as Mr. Salvador has let us clearly
understand his, I shall also examine the question under a merely
human point of view, and proceed to inquire, with him, "Whether
Jesus Christ, considered as a *simple citizen,* was tried according to the
existing laws and formalities."

The Catholic religion itself warrants me in this; it is not a mere
fiction; for God willed, that Jesus should be clothed in the forms of
humanity (*et homo factus est*), and that he should undergo the lot and
sufferings of humanity. The son of *God,* as to his moral state and his
holy spirit, he was also, in reality, the *Son of Man,* for the purpose of
accomplishing the mission which he came upon earth to fulfill.

This being the state of the question, then, I enter upon my subject; and I do not hesitate to affirm, because I will prove it, that,
upon examining all the circumstances of this great trial, we shall be
very far from discovering in it the application of those legal maxims
which are the safeguard of the rights of accused persons, and of
which Mr. Salvador, in his chapter "On the Administration of Justice," has made a seductive exposition.

The accusation of Jesus, instigated by the hatred of the priests and
the Pharisees, and presented at first as a charge of *sacrilege,* but
afterwards converted into *political* crime and an *offence against the
state,* was marked, in all its aspects, with the foulest acts of violence
and perfidy. It was not so much a *trial* environed with legal forms, as
a real *passion,* or prolonged suffering, in which the imperturbable
gentleness of the victim displays more strongly the unrelenting feroc-
ity of his persecutors.

When Jesus appeared among the Jews, that people was but the
shadow of itself. Broken down by more than one subjugation, divided

by factions and irreconcilable sects, they had in the last resort been obliged to succumb to the Roman power and surrender their own sovereignty. Jerusalem, having become a mere appendage to the province of Syria, saw within its walls an imperial garrison; Pilate commanded there, in the name of Caesar; and the late people of God were groaning under the double tyranny of a conqueror, whose power they abhorred and whose idolatry they detested, and of a priesthood that exerted itself to keep them under the rigorous bonds of a religious fanaticism.

Jesus Christ deplored the misfortunes of his country. How often did he weep for Jerusalem! Read in Bossuet's *Politics drawn from the Holy Scriptures,* the admirable chapter entitled, "Jesus Christ the good citizen." He recommended to his countrymen *union,* which constitutes the strength of states. "O Jerusalem, Jerusalem," said he, "thou that killest the prophets and stonest them which are sent unto thee, how often would I have gathered thy children together, even as a hen gathereth her chickens under her wings, and ye would not!"

He was supposed to be not favorable to the Romans; but he only loved his own countrymen more. Witness the address of the Jews, who, in order to induce him to restore to the centurion a sick servant that was dear to him, used as the most powerful argument these words—"'that he was worthy for whom he should do this, for he loveth our nation.' . . . And Jesus went with them" (Luke 7:4–5).

Touched with the distresses of the nation, Jesus comforted them by holding up to them the hope of another life; he alarmed the great, the rich, and the haughty, by the prospect of a final judgment at which every man would be judged not according to his rank, but his works. He was desirous of again bringing back man to his original dignity; he spoke to him of his *duties,* but at the same time of his *rights.* The people heard him with avidity, and followed him with eagerness; his words affected them; his hand healed their diseases, and his moral teaching instructed them; he preached, and practiced one virtue till then unknown, and which belongs to him alone— *charity.* This celebrity, however, and these wonders excited envy. The partisans of the *ancient theocracy* were alarmed at the *new doctrine;*

the chief priests felt that their power was threatened; the pride of the Pharisees was humbled; the scribes came in as their auxiliaries, and the destruction of Jesus was resolved upon.

Now, if his conduct was reprehensible, if it afforded grounds for a *legal accusation,* why was not that course taken openly? Why not try him for the acts committed by him, and for his public discourses? Why employ against him subterfuges, artifice, betrayal, and violence? for such was the mode of proceeding against Jesus.

Let us now take up the subject, and look at the narratives which have come down to us. Let us, with Mr. Salvador, open the books of the Gospels; for he does not object to that testimony; nay, he relies upon it: "It is by the Gospels themselves," says he, "that I shall establish *all the facts.*"

In truth, how can we (except by contrary evidence, of which there is none) refuse to place confidence in an historian, who tells us, as Saint John does, with affecting simplicity: "He that saw it bare record, and his record is true; and he knoweth that he saith true, that ye might believe" (John 19:35).

Section 1
Spies, or Informers

Who will not be surprised to find in this case the odious practice of employing *hired informers?* Branded with infamy, as they are in modern times, they will be still more so when we carry back their origin to the trial of Christ. It will be seen presently, whether I have not properly characterized by the name of *hired informers,* those emissaries, whom of the chief priests sent out to be about Jesus.

We read in the evangelist Luke 20:20: *Et observantes miserunt insidiatores, qui se justos simularent, ut caperent eum in sermone, et traderent illum principatui et potestati praesidis.* I will not translate this text myself, but will take the language of a translator whose accuracy is well known, Mr. De Sacy: "As they only sought occasions for his destruction, they sent to him *apostate persons* who *feigned themselves just men,* in order to *take hold* of his words, that they might deliver him unto the magistrate and into the power of the governor." And

Mr. De Sacy adds—"if there should escape from him the least word against the public authorities."

This first article has escaped the sagacity of Mr. Salvador.

Section 2
The Corruption and Treachery of Judas

According to Mr. Salvador, the senate, as he calls it, did not commence their proceedings by arresting Jesus, as would be done at the present day; but they began by passing a preliminary decree, that he should be arrested; and he cites, in proof of his assertion, John 11:53–54, and Matthew 26:4–5.

But John says nothing of this pretended decree. He speaks, too, not of a public sitting, but of a consultation held by the chief priests and the *Pharisees*, who did not, to my knowledge, constitute a judicial tribunal among the Jews. "Then gathered the chief priests and the Pharisees a council, and said, What do we? for this man *doeth many miracles*" (John 11:47). They add: "If we let him thus alone, all men will believe on him,"—which imported also, in their minds, *and they will no longer believe in us.* Now, in this, I can readily perceive the fear of seeing the morals and doctrines of Jesus prevail; but where is the preliminary *judgment,* or decree? I cannot discover it.

"And one of them named Caiaphas, being the high priest that same year, said unto them, Ye know nothing at all, nor consider, that it is expedient for us, that one man should die for the people . . . and he *prophesied,* that Jesus should die for the nation of the Jews." But to *prophesy* is not to *pass judgment;* and the *individual* opinion of Caiaphas, who was only one among them, was not the opinion of all, nor a *judgment of the senate.* We, therefore, still find a *judgment* wanting; and we only observe, that the priests and Pharisees are stimulated by a violent hatred of Jesus, and that "from that day forth they took counsel together for *to put him to death; ut interficerent eum*" (John 11:53).

The authority of St. John, then, is directly in contradiction of the assertion that there was an *order of arrest* previously passed by a regular tribunal.

Matthew, in relating the same facts, says that the chief priests assembled at the palace of the high priest, who was called Caiaphas, and there held counsel together. But what counsel? and what was the result of it? Was it to issue an *order of arrest* against Jesus, that they might hear him and then pass sentence? Not at all; but they held counsel together, "that they might take Jesus *by subtilty*, or *fraud*, and *kill him; concilium fercerunt, ut Jesum DOLO tenerent et OCCIDERENT"* (Matt. 26:5). Now in the Latin language, a language perfectly well constituted in everything relating to terms of the law, the words *occidere* and *interficere* were never employed to express the act of passing *sentence* or *judgment of death*, but simply to signify *murder* or *assassination*.[4]

This fraud, by the aid of which they were to get Jesus into their power, was nothing but the bargain made between the chief priests and Judas.

Judas, one of the twelve, goes to find the chief priests, and says to them, "What will ye give me, and I will deliver him unto you?" (Matt. 26:14–15). And they covenanted with him for thirty pieces of silver! Jesus who foresaw his treachery, warned him of it mildly, in the midst of the Last Supper, where the voice of his master, in the presence of his brethren, should have touched him and awakened his reflections! But not so; wholly absorbed in his reward, Judas placed himself at the head of a gang of servants, to whom he was to point out Jesus; and, then, by a *kiss* consummated his treachery![5]

Is it thus that a *judicial decree was to be executed*, if there had really been one made for the arrest of Jesus?

Section 3
Personal Liberty—Resistance to an Armed Force

The act was done in the *night time*. After having celebrated the Supper, Jesus had conducted his disciples to Mount of Olives. He prayed fervently; but they fell asleep.

Jesus awakes them, with a gentle reproof for their weakness, and warns them that the moment is approaching. "Rise, let us be going; behold he is at hand that doth betray me" (Matt. 26:46).

Judas was not alone; in his suite there was a kind of ruffian band, almost entirely composed of servants of the high priest, but whom

Mr. Salvador honors with the title of the *legal soldiery*. If in the crowd there were any Roman *soldiers*, they were there as spectators, and without having been legally called on duty; for the Roman commanding officer, Pilate, had not yet heard the affair spoken of.

This personal seizure of Jesus had so much the appearance of a forcible arrest, an illegal act of violence, that his disciples made preparation to repel by force.

Malchus, the insolent servant of the high priest, having shown himself the most eager to rush upon Jesus, Peter, not less zealous for his own master, cut off the servant's right ear.

This resistance might have been continued with success if Jesus had not immediately interfered. But what proves that Peter, even while causing bloodshed, was not resisting a *legal order*, a *legal judgment* or decree, (which would have made his resistance an act of *rebellion by an armed force against a judicial order*,) is this—that he was not arrested, either at the moment or afterwards, at the house of the high priest, to which he followed Jesus, and where he was most distinctly recognized by the maid servant of the high priest, and even by a relative of Malchus.

Jesus alone was arrested; and although he had not individually offered any active resistance, and had even restrained that of his disciples, they bound him as a malefactor; which was a criminal degree of rigor, since for the purpose of securing a single man by a numerous band of persons armed with swords and staves it was not necessary. "Be ye come out as against a thief with swords and staves?" (Luke 22:52).

Section 4
Other Irregularities in the Arrest—
Seizure of the Person

They dragged Jesus along with them; and, instead of taking him directly to the proper magistrate, they carried him before Annas, who had no other character than that of being *father-in-law* to the high priest (John 18:13). Now, if this was only for the purpose of letting him be seen by him, such a curiosity was not to be gratified; it was a vexatious proceeding, an irregularity.

From the house of Annas they led him to that of the high priest; all the time being *bound* (John 18:24). They placed him in the court yard; it was cold, and they made a fire; it was in the night time, but by the light of the light of the fire Peter was recognized by the people of the palace.

Now the Jewish law prohibited *all proceedings by night;* here, therefore, there was another infraction of the law.

Under this state of things, his person being forcibly seized and detained in a private house, and delivered into the hands of servants, in the midst of a court, how was Jesus treated? St. Luke says, "the men that held Jesus *mocked* him and *smote* him; and when they had blindfolded him, they struck him on the face, and asked him, saying, Prophesy, who is it that smote thee? And many other things blasphemously spake they against him" (Luke 22:63–65).

Will it be said, as Mr. Salvador does, that all this took place out of the presence of the senate? Let us wait, in this instance, till the senate shall be called up, and we shall see how far they protected the accused person.

Section 5
Captious Interrogatories—
Acts of Violence towards Jesus

Already had the cock crowed! But it was not yet day. The elders of the people and the chief priests and the scribes came together, and, having caused Jesus to appeal before their council, they proceeded to interrogate him (Luke 22:66).

Now, in the outset, it should be observed, that if they had been less carried away by their hatred, they should, as it was the *night time,* not only have postponed, but put a stop to the proceedings, because it was the *feast of the Passover,* the most solemn of all festivals; and according to their law no *judicial procedure* could take place on a feast-day, under the penalty of being null.[6] Nevertheless, let us see who proceeded to interrogate Jesus. This was that same Caiaphas, who, if he had intended to remain a *judge,* was evidently liable to objection; for in the preceding assemblage he had made himself the *accuser* of Jesus.[7] Even before he had seen or heard him, he declared him to be *deserving of death*. He said to his colleagues, that "it was *expedient* that one man should die for all" (John 18:14). Such being the opinion of Caiaphas, we shall not be surprised, if he shows partiality.

Instead of interrogating Jesus respecting *positive acts done*, with their circumstances, and respecting *facts personal to himself*, Caiaphas interrogates him respecting *general facts*, respecting his disciples (whom it would have been much more simple to have called as witnesses), and respecting his *doctrine*, which was a mere abstraction so long as no external acts were the consequence of it. "The high priest then asked Jesus of his disciples and of his doctrine" (John 18:19).

Jesus answered with dignity: "I spake openly to the world; I ever taught in the synagogue and in the temple, whither the Jews always resort; and in secret have I said nothing" (v. 20).

"Why asketh thou me? Ask them which heard me, *what I have said unto them;* behold, they know what I said" (v. 21).

"And when he had thus spoken, one of the officers which stood by struck Jesus with the palm of his hand, saying, Answerest thou the high priest so?" (v. 21).

Will it here be still said, that this violence was the individual act of the person who thus struck the accused? I answer, that on this occasion the fact took place in the presence and under the eyes of the whole council; and, as the high priest who presided did not restrain the author of it, I come to the conclusion, that he became an accomplice, especially when this violence was committed under the pretence of avenging the alleged affront to his dignity.

But in what respect could the answer of Jesus appear offensive? "If I have spoken evil," said Jesus, "bear witness of the evil but if well, why smitest thou me?"[8] (John 18:23).

There remained no mode of escaping from this dilemma. They accused Jesus; it was for those, who accused, to prove their accusation. An accused person is not obliged to criminate himself. He should have been convicted by proofs; he himself called for them. Let us see what witnesses were produced against him.

Section 6
Witnesses—New Interrogatories—
The Judge in a Passion

"And the chief priests and all the council sought for witness against Jesus to put him to death; and found none" (Mark 14:55).

"For many bare *false witness* against him, but their witness agreed not together" (v. 56).

"And there arose certain, and bare false witness against him, saying, We heard him say, I will destroy this temple that is made with hands, and within three days I will build another made without hands" (vv. 57–58).

"But (to the same point still) neither so did their witness agree together" (v. 59).

Mr. Salvador, on this subject, says, "The two witnesses, whom Matthew and Mark charge with *falsehood*, narrate a discourse which John declares to be *true*, so far as respects the power which Jesus Christ attributes to himself."

This alleged contradiction among the Evangelists does not exist. In the first place, Matthew does not say that the discourse was had by Jesus. In 26:61, he states the depositions of the witnesses, but saying at the same time that they were *false witnesses*; and in 27:40, he put the same declaration into the mouths of those who insulted Jesus at the foot of the cross; but he does not put it into the mouth of Christ. He is in accordance with Mark.

John 2:19 makes Jesus speak in these words: "Jesus answered and said unto them, Destroy this temple, and in three days I will raise it up." And John adds: "He spake of the temple of his body."

Thus Jesus did not say in an affirmative and somewhat menacing manner, *I will destroy this temple,* as the witnesses *falsely* assumed; he only said, hypothetically, *Destroy this temple,* that is to say, suppose this temple should be destroyed, I will raise it up in three days. Besides, they could not dissemble, that he referred to a temple altogether different from theirs, because he said, I will raise up another in three days, *which will not be made by the hands of man.*

It hence results, at least, that the Jews did not understand him, for they cried out, "Forty and six years was this temple in building, and wilt thou rear it up in three days?"

Thus, then, the witnesses did not agree together, and their declarations had nothing conclusive (Mark 14:59). We must, therefore, look for other proofs.

"Then the high priest, (we must not forget that he is still the accuser,) stood up in the midst, and asked Jesus, saying, Answerest thou nothing? what is it, which these witness against thee? But he held his peace, and answered nothing" (Mark 14:60–61). In truth, since the question was not concerning the temple of the Jews, but an ideal temple, not made by the hand of man, and which was alone in the thoughts of Jesus, the explanation was to be found in the very evidence itself.

The high priest continued: "I adjure thee, by the living God, that thou tell us, whether thou be the Christ, the Son of God" (Matt. 26:63). I adjure thee, I call upon thee on oath! a gross infraction of that rule of morals and jurisprudence, which forbids our placing an accused person between the danger of perjury and the fear of inculpating himself, and thus making his situation more hazardous. The high priest, however, persists, and says to him: Art thou the Christ, the Son of God?[9] Jesus answered, *Thou hast said* (Matthew 26:64); *I am* (Mark 14:62).

"Then the high priest rent his clothes, saying, *He hath spoken blasphemy; what further need have we of witnesses?* behold, now *ye have heard his blasphemy.* What think ye? They answered and said, He is guilty of death" (Matt. 26:65–66).

Let us now compare this scene of violence with the mild deduction of principles, which we find in the chapter of Mr. Salvador "On the Administration of Justice"; and let us ask ourselves, if, as he alleges, we find a just *application* of them in the proceedings against Christ?

Do we discover here that *respect* of the Hebrew judge towards the party accused, when we see that Caiaphas permitted him to be struck, in his presence, *with impunity?*

What was this Caiaphas, at once an accuser and judge?[10] A passionate man, and too much resembling the odious portrait which the historian Josephus has given us of him![11] A judge, who was irritated to such a degree, that he rent his clothes; who imposed upon the accused a most solemn oath, and who gave to his answers the criminal character, that *he had spoken* blasphemy! And, from that moment, he wanted no more witnesses, notwithstanding the law required them. He would not have an inquiry, which he perceived would be insufficient; he attempts to supply it by captious questions. He is desirous of having him condemned *upon his own declaration alone,* (interpreted, too, as he chooses to understand it,) though that was forbidden by the laws of the Hebrews! And, in the midst of a most violent transport of passion, this accuser himself a high priest, who means to speak in the name of the living God, is the first to pass sentence of death, and carries with him the opinions of the rest!

In this hideous picture I cannot recognize that justice of the Hebrews, of which Mr. Salvador has given a fine view in *his theory!*

Section 7
Subsequent Acts of Violence

Immediately after this kind of sacerdotal verdict rendered against Jesus, the acts of violence and insults began again with increased strength; the fury of the judge must have communicated itself to the bystanders. St. Matthew says: "Then did they spit in his face, and buffeted him; and others smote him with the palms of their hands, saying, Prophesy unto us, thou Christ; who is he that smote thee?" (Matt. 26:67–68).

Mr. Salvador does not contest the truth of this ill treatment. He says, "It was contrary to the spirit of the Hebrew law, and that it was not according to the order of nature, that a senate composed of the most respectable men of a nation,—that a senate, which, might perhaps be mistaken, but which thought it was acting mildly, should have permitted such outrages against him whose life it held in its own hands. The writers, who have transmitted these details to us, not having been present themselves at the trial, were disposed to overcharge the picture, either on account of their own feelings, or to throw upon their judges a greater odium."

I repeat; this ill treatment was entirely contrary to the spirit of the law. And what do I want more, since my object is to make prominent *all the violations of law.*

"It is not in nature to see a body, which respects itself, authorize such attempts." But of what consequence is that, when the fact is established? "The historians, it is said, were not present at the trial." But was Mr. Salvador there present himself, so that he could give a flat denial of their statements And when even an able writer, who was not an eye-witness, relates the same events after the lapse of more than eighteen centuries, he ought at least to bring opposing evidence, if he would impeach that of contemporaries; who, if they were not in the very hall of the council, were certainly on the spot, in the vicinity, perhaps in the court yard, inquiring anxiously of every thing that was happening to the man whose disciples they were.[12] Besides, the learned author whom I am combating says, in the outset, it is from the Gospels themselves that he will take all his facts. He must then take the whole together, as well those which go to condemn, as those which are in mitigation or excuse.

Those gross insults, those inhuman acts of violence, even if they are to be cast upon the servants of the high priest and the persons in his train, do not excuse those individuals, who, when they took upon themselves the authority of judges, were bound at the same time to throw around him all the protection of the law. Caiaphas, too, was guilty as the master of the house (for every thing took place in his house), even if he should not be responsible as high priest and president of the council for having permitted excesses, which, indeed were but too much in accordance with the rage he had himself displayed upon the bench.

These outrages, which would be inexcusable even towards a man irrevocably condemned to punishment, were the more criminal towards Jesus, because, legally and judicially speaking, there had not yet been any sentence properly passed against him according to the public law of the country; as we shall see in the following section, which will deserve the undivided attention of the reader.

Section 8
The Position of the
Jews in respect to the Romans

We must not forget, *that Judea was a conquered country.* After the death of Herod most inappropriately surnamed *the Great*—Augustus had confirmed his last will, by which that king of the Jews had arranged the division of his dominions between *his* two sons: but Augustus did not continue their title of *king,* which their father had borne.

Archelaus, on whom Judea devolved, having been recalled on account of his cruelties, the territory, which was at first intrusted to his command, was united to the province of Syria (Josephus, *Antiq. Jud.* lib. 17, cap. 15).

Augustus then appointed particular officers for Judea. Tiberius did the same; and at the time of which we are speaking, Pilate was one of those officers (Josephus, *Antiq.* lib. 18, cap. 3, 8).

Some have considered Pilate as governor, by title, and have given him the Latin appellation *Praeses,* president or governor. But they have mistaken the force of the word. Pilate was one of those public officers, who were called by the Romans, *procurator Caesaris,* Imperial procurators.

With this title of *procurator,* he was placed under the superior authority of the governor of Syria, the true *praeses,* or governor of that province, of which Judea was then only one of the dependencies.

To the governor (*praeses*) peculiarly belonged the right of taking cognizance of *capital* cases.[13] The *procurator,* on the contrary, had, for his principal duty, nothing but the collection of the revenue, and the trial of revenue causes. But the right of taking cognizance of *capital* cases did, in some instances, belong to certain *procurators,* who were sent into small provinces to fill the places of governors (*vice-praesides*), as appears clearly from the Roman laws.[14] Such was *Pilate* at Jerusalem.[15]

The Jews, placed in political position—notwithstanding they were left in the enjoyment of their civil laws, the public exercise of their religion, and many things merely relating to their police and municipal regulations—the Jews, I say, had not the *power of life and death;* this was a principle attribute of sovereignty, which the Romans always took great care to reserve to themselves, even if they neglected other things. *Apud Romanos, jus valet gladii; caetera transmittuntur* (Tacitus).

What then was the right of the Jewish authorities in regard to Jesus? Without doubt the scribes, and their friends the Pharisees, might well have been alarmed, as a body and individually, at the preaching and success of Jesus; they might be concerned for their worship; and they might have interrogated the man respecting his creed and his doctrines,—they might have made a kind of preparatory proceeding, they might have declared, in point of fact, that those doctrines, which threatened their own, were contrary to their law, as understood by themselves.

But this law, although it had not undergone any alteration as to the affairs of religion, had no longer any coercive power as to the external or civil regulations of society. In vain would they have undertaken to pronounce sentence of death under the circumstances of the case of Jesus; the council of the Jews had not the power to pass a *sentence of death;* it only would have hid power to make *an accusation* against him before the governor, or his deputy, and then deliver him over to be tried by him.

Let us distinctly establish this point; for here I entirely differ in opinion from Mr. Salvador. According to him, "the Jews had *reserved the power of trying, according to their law;* but it was in the hands of the *procurator* alone, that the executive power was vested; every culprit must be put to death by *his consent,* in order that the senate should not have the means of reaching persons that were sold to foreigners."

No; the Jews had not reserved *the right of passing sentence of death.* This right had been transferred to the Romans by the very act of conquest and this was not merely that the senate should not have the means of reaching persons who were sold to foreign countries, but it was done in order that the conqueror might be able to reach those individuals who should become *impatient of the yoke;* it was, in short, for the equal protection of all, as all had become Roman subjects and to Rome alone belonged the highest judicial power which is the principal attribute of sovereignty. Pilate, as the representative of Caesar in Judea, was not merely an agent of the *executive authority,* which would have left the *judiciary* and *legislative* power in the hands of the conquered people—he was not simply an officer appointed to give an *exequatur* or mere approval (*visa*) to sentences passed by *another authority,* the *authority of the Jews.* When the matter in question was a capital case, the Roman authorities not only ordered the *execution* of a sentence, but also took cognizance (*cognitio*) of the crime; it had the right of jurisdiction *a priori,* and that of *passing judgment in the last resort.* If Pilate himself had not had this power by special delegation, *vice praesidis,* it was vested in the governor, within whose territorial jurisdiction the case occured; but in any event we hold it to be clear, that the Jews had lost the right of *condemning to death* any person whatever, not only so far as respects the *execution* but the *passing* of the sentence. This is one of the best settled points in the provincial law of the Romans.

The Jews were not ignorant of this; for when they went before Pilate, to ask of him the condemnation of Jesus, they themselves declared, that it was not permitted to them to put any person to death: "It is not lawful for us to put any man to death" (John 18:31).

Here I am happy to be able to support myself by the opinion of a very respectable authority, the celebrated Loiseau, in his treatise on *Seigneuries,* in the chapter on the administration of *justice belonging to cities.* "In truth," says he, "there is some evidence, that the *police,* in which the people had the sole interest, was administered by officers of the people; but I know not upon what were founded the concession of power to some cities of France to exercise criminal jurisdiction; nor why the Ordinance of Moulins left that to them rather than civil cases; for the criminal jurisdiction is the *right of the sword,* the *merum imperium,* or absolute sovereignty. Accordingly, by the Roman law, the administration of justice was so far prohibited to the officers of cities, that they could not punish even by a simple fine. *Thus it is doubtless that we must understand* that passage of the Gospel, where the Jews say to Pilate, *It is not lawful for us to put any man to death;* for, after they were subjected to the Romans, they had not jurisdiciton of crimes."

Let us now follow Jesus to the presence of Pilate.

Section 9
The Accusation made before Pilate

At this point I must entreat the particular attention of the reader. The irregularities and acts of violence, which I have hitherto remarked upon, are nothing in comparison with the unbridled fury which is about to display itself before the *Roman judge,* in order to extort from him, against his own conviction, a sentence of death.

"And straightway in the morning the chief priests held a consultation with the elders, and scribes, and the whole council, and bound Jesus, and carried him away, and delivered him to Pilate" (Mark 15:1).

As soon as the morning was come; for, as I have observed already, every thing which had been done thus far against Jesus was done *during the night.*

They then led Jesus from Caiaphas to the Hall of Judgment of Pilate.[16] It was early; and they themselves went not into the judgment hall, *lest they should be defiled;* but that they might eat the passover (John 18:28).

Singular scrupulousness! and truly worthy of the Pharisees! They were afraid of *defiling themselves on the day of the passover* by entering *the house* of a heathen! And, yet, the same day, only some hours before presenting themselves to Pilate, they had, in contempt of their own law, committed the outrage of *holding a council* and deliberating upon *an accusation of a capital crime.*

As they would not enter, "Pilate went out to them" (John 18:29). Now observe his language. He did not say to them, *Where is the sentence you have passed;* as he must have done, if he was only to give them his simple *exequatur,* or permission to execute the sentence; but he takes up the matter from the beginning, as would be done by one who had *plenary jurisdiction;* and he says to them: "What accusation bring ye against this man?"

They answered, with their accustomed haughtiness: "If he were not a *malefactor,* we would not have delivered him up unto thee"

(John 18:30). They wished to have it understood that, being a question of *blasphemy*, it was the *cause of their religion*, which they could appreciate better than any others could. Pilate, then, would have been under the necessity of believing them *on their word*. But this Roman, indignant at their porposed course of proceeding, which would have restricted his jurisdiction by making him the passive instrument of the wishes of the Jews, answered them in an ironical manner: Well, since you say he has sinned against your law, take him yourselves and judge him according to your law (John 18:31). This was an absolute mystification to them, for they knew their own want of power to condemn him to death. But they were obliged to yield the point, and to submit to Pilate himself their *articles of accusation*.

Now what were the grounds of this accusation? Were they *the same* which had hitherto been alleged against Jesus—the charge of *blasphemy*—which was the only one brought forward by Caiaphas before the council of the Jews? Not at all; despairing of obtaining from the Roman judge a sentence of *death* for a *religious* quarrel, which was of no interest to the Romans,[17] they suddenly changed their plan; they abandoned their first accusation, the charge of blasphemy, and subtituted for it a *political* accusation, *an offence against the state*.

Here we have the very crisis, or essential incident, of the passion; and that which makes the heaviest accusation of guilt on the part of the informers against Jesus. For, being fully bent on destroying him in any manner whatever, they no longer exhibited themselves as the avengers of *their religion*, which was alleged to have been outraged, or of their worship, which it was pretended was threatened; but, ceasing to appear as Jews, in order to affect sentiments belonging to a foreign nation, those hypocrites held out the appearance of being concerned for the interests of *Rome*, they accused their own countryman of an intention to restore the kingdom of Jerusalem, to make himself *king* of the *Jews*, and to make an insurrection of the people against their conquerors. Let us hear them speak for themselves:

"And they began to *accuse* him saying, We found this fellow perverting the nation, and forbidding to give tribute to Caesar, saying, that he himself is Christ a *king*" (Luke 23:2).

What a calumny! Jesus forbidding to give tribute to Caesar! when he had answered the Pharisees themselves, in presence of the whole people, by showing them the image of Caesar upon a Roman piece of money, and saying, Give unto Caesar the things which are Caesar's. But this accusation was one mode of intereting Pilate in respect to his jurisdiction; for, as an imperial *procurator*, he was specially to supervised the collection of the revenue. The second branch of the accusation still more direclty affected the sovereignty of the Romans: "He holds himself up for a *king.*"

The accusation having thus assumed a character purely *political,* Pilate thought he must pay attention to it. "Then Pilate entered into the judgment hall," (the place where justice was administered), and having *summoned Jesus to appear* before him, he proceeds to his examination, and says to him: "Art thou the king of the Jews?" (John 18:33).

This question, so different from those which had been addressed to him at the house of the high priest, appears to have excited the astonishment of Jesus; and, in his turn, he asked Pilate: "Sayest thou this thing of thyself, or did others tell it thee of me?" (v. 24). In reality, Jesus was desirous of knowing, first of all, the authors of this new accusation—Is this an accusation brought against me by the *Romans* or by the *Jews?*

Pilate replied to him—"Am I a Jew? Thine own nation and the chief priests have delivered thee unto me; what hast thou done?" (v. 35).

All the particulars of this procedure are important; I can not too often repeat the remark, that in no part of the transactions before Pilate is there any question at all respecting a previous sentence, a judgment already passed—a judgment, the execution of which was the only subject of consideration; it was a case of a capital accusation; but an accusation which was then just beginning; they were about the preliminary interrogatories put to the accused, and Pilate says to him, "What hast thou done?"

Jesus, seeing by the explanation what was the source of the *prejudging* of his case, and knowing the secret thoughts which predominated in making the accusation, and that his enemies wanted to arrive at the same end by an artifice, answered Pilate—"*My kingdom is not of this world;* if my kingdom were of this world, then would my servants fight, that I should not be delivered to the Jews;" we see, in fact, that Jesus had forbidden his people to resist; but, he added, "now is my kingdom not from hence" (John 18:36).

This answer of Jesus is very remarkable; it became the foundation of his religion, and the pledge of its universality, because it detached it from the interests of all governments. It rests not merely in assertion, in doctrine; it was given in *justification*, in *defense* against the accusation of intending to make himself *king of the Jews*. Indeed, if Jesus had affected a *temporal* royal authority, if there had been the least attempt, on his part, to usurp the *power of Caesar*, he would have been guilty of treason in the eyes of the magistrate. But, by answering twice, my *kingdom is not of this world*, my kingdom is not from hence, his justification was complete.

Pilate, however, persisted and said to him: "Art thou a king then?" Jesus replied, "Thou sayest that I am a king. To this end was I born, and for this cause came I into the world, that I should bear witness unto the truth. Every one that is of the truth heareth my voice" (John 18:37).

Pilate then said to him: *What is the truth?*

This question proves that Pilate had not a very clear idea of what Jesus called *the truth*. He perceived nothing in it but *ideology*; and, satisfied with having said (less in the manner of a question than of an exclamation) "*What is the truth,*" he went to the Jews (who remained outside) and said to them, "*I find in him no fault at all*" (John 18:38).

Here, then, we see Jesus absolved from the accusation by the declaration of the Roman judge himself.

But the accusers, persisting still farther, added—"*He stirreth up the people, teaching* throughout all Jewry, beginning from Galilee to this place*" (Luke 23:5).

"He stirreth up the people!" This is a charge of sedition; and for Pilate. But observe, it was *by the doctrine which he teaches;* these words comprehended the real complaint of the Jews. To them it was equivalent to saying—He *teaches* the people, he instructs them, he enlightens them; he preaches *new doctrines* which are not *ours*. "He stirs up the people!" This, in their mouth signified—the people hear him willingly; the people follow and become attached to him; for he preaches a doctrine that is friendly and consolatory to the people; he unmasks our pride, our avarice, our insatiable spirit of domination!

Pilate, however, does not appear to have attached much importance to this new turn given to the accusation; but he here betrays a weakness. He heard the word *Galilee*, and he makes that the occasion of shifting off the responsibility upon another public officer, and seizes the occasion with avidity. He says to Jesus—you are a *Galilean* then? and, upon the answer being in the affirmative, considering Jesus as belonging to the jurisdiciton of Herod-Antipas, who, by the good pleasure of Caesar, was then tetrarch of Galilee, he sent him to Herod (Luke 23:6–7).

But Herod, who, as St. Luke says, had been long desirous of *seeing Jesus* and had hoped to see *some miracle* done by him, after satisfying an idle curiosity and putting several questions to him, which Jesus did not deign to answer,—Herod notwithstanding the presence of the priests, (who had not yet gone off, but stood there with their scribes,) and notwithstanding the pertinacity with which they continued to accuse Jesus, perceiving nothing but what was merely fanciful in the *accusation of being a king*, made a mockery of the affair, and sent Jesus back to Pilate, *after having arrayed him in a gorgeous robe,* in order to show that he thought this pretended royalty was a subject of ridicule rather than of apprehension (Luke 23:8ff. and De Sacy. Ib.).

Section 10
The Last Efforts before Pilate

No person, then, was willing to condemn Jesus; neither Herod, who only made the case a subject of mockery, nor Pilate, who had openly declared that he found nothing criminal in him.

But the hatred of the priests was not disarmed; so far from it, that the chief priests, with a numerous train of their partisans, returned to Pilate with a determination to force him to a decision.

The unfortunate Pilate, reviewing his proceedings in their presence, said to them again: "Ye have brought this man unto me as one that perverteth the people: and behold, I, having examined him before you, *have found no fault in this man touching those things whereof ye accuse him:* No, nor yet Herod; for I sent you to him, and lo, *nothing worthy of death is done unto him.* I will therefore chastise him and release him" (Luke 23:14–15).

After "chastising" him! And was not this a piece of cruelty, when he considered him to be innocent?[18] But this was an act of condescension by which Pilate hoped to quiet the rage with which he saw they were agitated.

"Then Pilate therefore took Jesus and scourged him" (John 19:1). And, supposing that he had done enough to disarm their fury, he exhibited him to them in that pitiable condition; Saying to them at the same time, Behold the man! *Ecce homo* (John 19:5).

Now, in my turn, I say, here is indeed a decree of Pilate; and an unjust decree; but it is not the pretended decree alleged to have been made by the Jews. It is a decision wholly different; an unjust decision, it is true; but sufficient to avail as *a legal bar* to any new proceedings against Jesus for the same act. *Non bis in idem,* no man shall be put twice in jeopardy, is a maxim, which has come down to us from the Romans.

Accordingly, "from thenceforth Pilate sought to *release* Jesus" (John 19:12).

Here, now, observe the deep perfidy of his accusers. "If thou let this man go, thou art not Caesar's friend; whosoever maketh himself a *king* speaketh against Caesar."

It does not appear that Pilate was malignant; we see all the efforts he had made at different times to save Jesus. But he was a *public officer,* and was attached to *his office;* he was intimidated by the outcry which called in question his *fidelity to the emperor;* he was afraid of a *dismissal;* and he yielded. He immediately reascended the judgment seat; and, as new light had thus come upon him, he proceeded to make a second decree!

But being for a moment stopped by the voice of his own conscience, and by the advice which his terrified wife sent to him—"*Have thou nothing to do with that just man*" (Matt. 27:19)—he made his last effort, by attempting to influence the populace to accept Barabbas instead of Jesus. "But the chief priests moved the people, that he should rather release Barabbas unto them" (Mark 15:11). Barabbas! a murderer! an assassin !

Pilate spoke to them again: *What will ye then that I should do with Jesus?* And they cried out, *Away with him, crucify him.* Pilate still persisted: *Shall I crucify your king?* thus using terms of mockery, in order to disarm them. But here showing themselves to be more truly Roman than Pilate himself, the chief priests hypocritically answered: *We have no king but Caesar* (John 19:15).

The outcry was renewed—Crucify him, crucify him! and the clamor became more and more threatening; "and the voices of them and of the chief priests prevailed" (Luke 23:23).

At length Pilate, *being desirous of pleasing the multitude,* proceeds to speak. But can we call it a legal adjudication, a *judgment,* that he is about to pronounce? Is he, at the moment, in that free state of mind which is necessary for a judge, who is about to pass a *sentence of death?* What new witnesses, what proofs have been brought forward to change his conviction and opinion which had been so energetically declared, of the innocence of Jesus?

"When Pilate saw that he could prevail nothing, but that rather a tumult was made, he took water and washed his hands before the multitude, Saying, *I am innocent of the blood of this just person; see ye to it*" (Matt. 27:24). "And Pilate gave sentence, that it should be as they required" (Luke 23:24). And "he delivered him to them to be crucified" (Matt. 27:26).

Well mayest thou wash thy hands, Pilate, stained as they are with innocent blood! Thou hast authorized the act in thy weakness; thou art not less culpable, than if thou hadst sacrificed him through wickedness! All generations, down to our own time, have repeated that the *Just One* suffered *under Pontius Pilate.* Thy name has remained in history, to serve for the instruction of all public men, all pusillanimous judges, in order to hold up to them the shame of *yielding contrary to one's own convictions.* The populace, in its fury, made an outcry at the foot of the judgment-seat, where, perhaps, thou thyself didst not sit securely! But of what importance was that? Thy *duty* spoke out; and in such a case, better would it be to suffer death, than to inflict it on another.[19]

We will now come to this conclusion.

The *proof* that Jesus was not, as Mr. Salvador maintains, put to death for the crime of blasphemy or sacrilege, and for having preached a new religious worship in contravention of the Mosaic law, results from the *very sentence,* pronounced by Pilate; a sentence, in pursuance of which he was led to execution by Roman soldiers.

There was among the Romans a custom, which was borrowed from their jurisprudence, and which is still followed, of placing over the head of a condemned criminal a writing containing *an extract from his sentence,* in order that the public might know *for what crime* he was condemned. This was the reason why Pilate put on the cross a label, on which he had written these words: *Jesus Nazarenus Rex Judaeorum,* (Jesus of Nazareth, King of the Jews), which has since been denoted by the initials J. N. R. J. This was the alleged cause of his condemnation. Mark says—"And the superscription of his *accusation* was written over—*The King of the Jews*" (Mark 15:26).

This inscription was first in *Latin,* which was the legal language of the *Roman* judge; and it was repeated in *Hebrew* and *Greek,* in order to be understood by the people of the nation and by foreigners.

The chief priests, whose indefatigable hatred did not overlook the most minute details, being apprehensive that people would take it to be literally a fact affirmed, that Jesus *was the King of the Jews,* said to Pilate: "Write not *King of the Jews,* but that *he said* I am king of the Jews." But Pilate answered: "What I have written I have written" (John 19:21–22).

This is a conclusive answer to one of the last assertions of Mr. Salvador, that "the Roman Pilate signed the sentence" by which he always means that Pilate did nothing but sign a sentence, which he supposes to have been passed by the Sanhedrin; but in this he is mistaken. Pilate did not merely *sign* the sentence, or decree, but *drew it up;* and, when his draft was objected to by the priests, he still adhered to it, saying, what I have written shall remain as written.

Here, then we see the true cause of the condemnation of Jesus?. Here, we have the "*judicial and legal* proof." Jesus was the victim of a *political* accusation! He was put to death for the imaginary crime of having aimed at the power of Caesar, by calling himself *King of the Jews!* Absurd accusation; which Pilate never believed, and which the chief priests and the Pharisees themselves did not believe. For they were not authorized to arrest Jesus on that account; it was a new, and totally different, accusation from that which they first planned a sudden accusation of the moment, when they saw that Pilate was but little affected by their *religious* zeal, and they found it necessary to arouse *his zeal for* Caesar.

"*If thou let this man go, thou art not Caesar's friend!*" This alarming language has too often, since that time, reverberated in the ears of timid judges, who, like Pilate, have rendered themselves criminal by delivering up victims through want of firmness whom they would never have condemned if they had listened to the voice of their own consciences.

Let us now recapitulate the case, as I have considered it from the beginning.

Is it not evident, contrary to the conclusion of Mr. Salvador, that Jesus considered merely as a *simple citizen*, was not tried and sentenced either *according to law, or agreeably to the form of legal proceedings then existing?*

God, according to his eternal design, might permit the just to suffer by the malice of men; but he also intended, that this should at least happen by a disregard of all laws, and by a violation of all established rules, in order that the entire contempt of forms should stand as the first warning of the violation of law.

Let us not be surprised then, that in another part of his work, Mr. Salvador (who, it is gratifying to observe, discusses his subject dispassionately) expresses some regret in speaking of the "*unfortunate sentence against Jesus*" (Vol. 1 p. 59). He has wished to excuse the Hebrews; but, one of that nation, in giving utterance to the feelings of his heart, still says—in language which I took from his his own mouth: "We should be very cautious of condemning him at this day."

I pass over the excesses which followed the order of Pilate; as, the violence shown to Simon, the Cyrenian, who was made in some degree a sharer in the punishment, by being compelled to carry the cross; the injurious treatment which attended the victim to the place of the sacrifice,[20] and even the cross, where Jesus still prayed for his brethren and his executioners!

To the heathen themselves I would say—You, who have gloried in the death of Socrates, how much must you be struck with wonder at that of Jesus! Ye, censors of the Areopagus, how could you undertake to excuse the Synagogue, and justify the sentence of the Hall of Judgment? Philosophy herself has not hesitated to proclaim, and we may repeat with her—"Yes, if the life and death of *Socrates* were those of a sage, the life and death of *Jesus* were those of a divinity."

Notes

1. This Analysis first appeared in the *Gazette des Tribunaux.*

2. Joshua 7:19ff.

3. By this, says Father Lamy, we may understand what the mixture of wine and myrrh was, which they presented to Jesus on the cross, and which he would not drink. *Introd. to the reading of the Holy Scriptures,* chap. 6 (Note of Mr. Salvador, Book 4 ch 2.)

4. As was that of Stephen, whom the same priests caused to be massacred by the populace, without a previous sentence of the law. Occidere: *Non occides,* thou shalt not kill (Deut. 5:17). *Veneno homines occidere.* Cic. pro Roscio, 61. *Virginiam filiam sua manu occidit Virginius.* Cic. de Finib. 107. *Non hominem occidi.* Horat. 1. Epist. 17, 10. *Inermem occidere.* Ovid. 2 Fast. 139. Interficere: *Feras interficere.* Lucret. lib. v. 251. Interfectus in acie. Cic. de Finib. 103. Caesaris interfectores. Brutus Ciceroni, 16, 8. *Interfectorem Gracchi.* Cic. de Claris Orrato. 66.

5. Will it be believed, that Tertullian and St. Irenaeus were obliged to refute seriously some writers of their day, who considered the conduct of Judas not only excusable, but worthy of admiration and highly meritorious "because of the immense service which he had rendered to the human race by *preparing their redemption*"! In the same manner, at a certain period, we have seen plunderers of the public money make a merit of their conduct, because in that way they had weakened the usurpation and prepared the way for the triumph of legitimacy.

6. See, as to these two grounds of nullity, the Jewish authors cited by Prost de Royer, tome 2, p. 205, *verbo* Accusation.

7. Mr. Salvador admits this: "Caiaphas," says he, "made himself his accuser".

8. Ananias, a chief priest, having given orders to strike Paul upon the face, Paul said to him: "God shall smite thee, thou whited wall; for sittest thou to judge me after the law, and commandest me to be smitten, *contrary to the law?*" (Acts 23:3).

9. Mr. Salvador, in his, admits, that "the expression *Son of God* was in common use among the Hebrews, to signify a man of great wisdom, or of

deep piety." But adds, "*It was not in this sense*, that it was used by Jesus Christ; it would not have caused so strong a sensation." Thus, then by *construction* and changing the words from their usual meaning, an article of accusation is formed against Jesus.

10. That is, he usurped the functions of a judge; for we shall see, in the next section, that the *council* of the Jews had not jurisdiction of capital cases.

11. Josephus, *Jewish Antiquities*. lib. 18. cap. 3, 6.

12. Peter followed him afar off unto the high priest's palace, and went in and sat with the servants to see the end (Matt. 26:58). So also the young man spoken of in Mark 14:51: "And there followed him a certain young man. . . ."

13. *De Crimine praesidis cognitio est.* Cujas, Observ. 19:13.

14. Procurator Caesaris *fungens vice praesidis* potest cognoscere *de causis criminalibus*. Godefroy, in his note (letter S) upon the 3rd law of the Code, *Ubi causae fiscales*. And he cites several others, which I have verified, and which are most precise to the same effect. See particularly the 4th law of the Code, *Ad leg. fab. de plag.*, and the 2nd law of the Code, *De Paenis*.

15. Procuratoribus Caesaris data est jurisdictio in causis fiscaslibus precuniariis, non in criminalibus, nisi quum fungebantur *vice praesidum;* ut Pontius Pilatus fuit procurator Caesaris *vice praesidis* in Syria. Cujas, Observ. 19:13.

16. "To carry one from Caiaphas to Pilate" has since become a proverb.

17. Lysias thus wrote to Felix the Governor, in relation to Paul: "Whom I perceived to be accused of questions of their law, but to have nothing laid to his charge worthy of death or bonds" (Acts 23:29).

18. Gerhard makes the following unanswerable dilemma upon this point. "Be consistent with thyself, Pilate; for, if Christ is innocent, why dost thou not send him away acquitted? And if thou believest him deserving of chastisement with rods, why dost thou proclaim him to be innocent?" *Gerh. Harm.* ch 193, p. 1889.

19. We will cite here the words of one of the finest laws of the Romans: Vane voces populi non sunt audiendae, quando aut noxium crimine absolvi, ant innocentem condemnari desiderant—The idle clamor of the populace is not to be regarded, when they call for a guilty man to be acquitted, or an innocent one to be condemned. *Law 12, Code de Paenis.* Pilate might also have read in Horace: Justum et tenacem—

> "The man in conscious virtue bold,
> Who dares his secret purpose hold,
> Unshaken hears the *crowd's* tumultuous cries,
> And the impetuous *tyrant's* angry brow defies."

20. "To the sufferings of those who were put to death were added mockery and derision" (Tacit. *Ann.* 15:44).

The Various Versions of the Bible

by Constantine Tischendorf

Not to mention earlier English versions, in the reign of Elizabeth, in the year 1568, the English nation received at the hands of the Bishops with Parker at their head, an authorized translation of the Bible. Fifty years later King James I ordered a revision to be undertaken by a select body of learned divines, and in this amended form it has continued until now in the hands of everybody as the Authorized Version. Formed from the original Greek text as it was in use among Protestant theologians in the days of Elizabeth and James the First, and executed with scholarship, conscientiousness, and love, this translation of the New Testament has not only become an object of great reverence but has deserved to be such. The English Church possesses in it a national treasure. Only the German Church inherits one equal to it in its New Testament by the hand of Luther. But the Greek text of the apostolic writings has, since its origin in the first century, experienced sundry vicissitudes in the hands of faithful men who have studied and made use of it; copies continually departed more and more from the first, and in this way numerous variations obtained currency. The English Authorized Version, equally with the Lutheran translation, is based upon the editions of the Greek text which Erasmus in 1516 and Robert Stephens in 1550 had founded upon manuscripts written after the tenth century. Whether those Greek copies out of which Erasmus and Stephens prepared their editions were altogether reliable, that is, whether they exhibited as far as possible the apostolic text, has long been matter of earnest discussion with the learned. Since the sixteenth century, Greek manuscripts have become known far older than those of Erasmus and Robert Stephens and besides the Greek, also Syriac, Egyptian, Latin, and Gothic, into which languages the original text was translated in the second, third, and fourth centuries; moreover, in the works of the Christian Fathers who wrote in the second and following centuries, many citations from texts of the New Testament have been found and compared.

What was the result? The learned saw, on the one hand, that the text of Erasmus and Stephens had been for the most part in use in the Byzantine national church long before the tenth century; but on the other hand, they learned the existence of thousands of readings which had not been edited by Erasmus and Stephens. Now the problem came to be, what reading in each instance most correctly represented that which the apostles had written. This problem is by no means an easy one for variations in the documents are very ancient; Jerome already notices them. Even in the fourth century there were diversities in very many places of the New Testament text. The learned have been and are very much divided in opinion as to which readings represent the Word of God most exactly; but one thing has been admitted by most who understand the matter, and it is that the oldest documents must come nearer to the original text than those that are later.

Providence has ordered it so that the New Testament can appeal to a far larger number of all kinds of original sources than the whole of the rest of ancient Greek literature. Before all others which it possesses, Christian scholars have for a long time highly valued two manuscripts, which to great antiquity add the distinction that they contain not merely more or fewer portions of the sacred text but the greater part of the entire New Testament as well as the Old. One of these manuscripts is deposited in the Vatican at Rome and the other in the British Museum. To these, within these ten years, a third has been added, brought from Mount Sinai and now at St. Petersburg. These three hold undoubtedly the first place among the many copies of the New Testament of a thousand years old and by their authority will have to be judged and rectified both the earlier Greek editions of the New Testament and all existing modern translations of it. Indeed it is to be hoped that out of them a Greek text will be prepared for the good of theological science in general and that it will be taken as the basis of new translations for the use of Christian churches everywhere.

Before this comes to pass, it is for all Christians, who highly value and esteem the Holy Scriptures of great interest, to learn to know the relation wherein the current European and American translations stand to the oldest copies of the original text of so great authority. And therefore it appeared to Baron Tauchnitz and to myself, as at once a work of piety and of learning, on the occasion of the thousandth volume of this collection, to present to English readers of the Bible an edition of the New Testament in which they would find, along with their authorized text, the readings which vary from it in the three most ancient and important manuscripts.

This comparison of the current English text with the most ancient authorities is fitted to draw attention to the degree in which these last confirm it, as well as to the frequency with which they deviate from it. It should not be forgotten, however, that the three manuscripts of which we speak differ among themselves both in age and importance and that not one of them stands so high as to exclude all gainsaying of its bare authority. But it would be either unwarrantable arrogance or blameworthy indolence to treat these primeval documents with neglect; it would be a misunderstanding of the dispensations of Providence, which have preserved these documents for fourteen or fifteen centuries, amid all the vicissitudes of time, and given them into our hands, if we were not ready most thankfully to give heed to them as instruments worthy of the highest respect for the recovery of the truth.

Is our undertaking by any possibility adverse to religion? May that which by long use for several centuries in churches and schools and houses has won respect and affection, be called in question as uncertain, and distrusted as inexact? He who should recognize irreligion in our testing and even calling into doubt that text of the Bible, respect for which simply results from common use, would greatly err. It seems to us much rather the greatest act of piety, to regard confidently as the Word of God, nothing which is not accredited and established as such by the most ancient and also most trustworthy evidences which the Lord has placed in our hands.

From this point of view and with this conviction, the writer of this introduction has for thirty years past explored the libraries of Europe, as well as the recesses of monasteries in the Asiatic and African East, in search of the most ancient copies of Holy Scripture; he has devoted his whole energy to collect all the most weighty documents of the kind, to labor upon them, to publish them for the benefit of posterity, and to restore on the basis of scientific research the very original text of the apostles. With the same conviction he has undertaken this popular task, this work upon the English New Testament. No nation has distinguished his labors and their happy results by so extensive a reception as the English, ever since he visited London, Oxford, and Cambridge for the first time a quarter of a century ago; he may hope, then, that the same nation will receive with genuine interest the book which we now place in its hands.

But before we proceed to speak of our indication of the various readings, it is but fitting that we should give a few more specific details about the three famous manuscripts which have been employed for the undertaking.

The Codex Vaticanus came first into the possession of learned Europe. From what place it came into the Vatican Library is not known, but it is entered in the very first catalogue of the collection dating from 1475. It contains the Old and New Testaments. Of the New it at present contains the four Gospels, the Acts, the seven General Epistles, nine of St. Paul's Epistles, and that to the Hebrews as far as Hebrews 9:14; but all that followed this place is lost, namely, the last chapters of the Hebrews, the two epistles to Timothy, the epistles to Titus and Philemon, and the Revelation. The text is written in three columns to a page. The peculiarity of the handwriting, the arrangement of the manuscript, and the character of the text itself, more especially certain remarkable readings, induce the opinion that the codex is to be referred to the fourth century and probably to about the middle of that century. During a long period the Roman Court very seldom granted access to the manuscript for any critical use of it, but in the year 1828, by the command of Pope Leo XII, the late Cardinal Angelo Mai undertook an edition of it. His edition first appeared in 1857, three years after his death, and was found to be full of mistakes. The writer of the present introduction corrected Mai's New Testament in several hundreds of passages in his *Novum Testamentum Vaticanum* published in 1867. Still further corrections are supplied in the facsimile edition of 1868 by Vercellone and Cozza (inserted also in the *Appendix Novi Testamenti Vaticani*, 1869).

The Codex Alexandrinus was sent in 1628 as a present to Charles I of England from Cyril Lucar, patriarch of Constantinople. Cyril Lucar, who had formerly been patriarch of Alexandria, brought it with him to Constantinople, and this explains why it is called the Alexandrian Codex. It is written in two columns to a page and contains the Old and New Testaments. It is imperfect in the New Testament, having lost Matthew 1:1–25; John 6:50–7:52, and 2 Corinthians 4:13–12:6. It contains, however, the two epistles by Clement of Rome which in it alone have descended to posterity, also an epistle of Athanasius, and a production by Eusebius on the Psalter. On paleographic and other grounds, it is believed to have been written in the middle of the fifth century. The New Testament was edited in 1786 by C. G. Woide and republished with corrections by B. Harris Cowper in an octavo edition issued in 1860.

I was so happy as to discover the Codex Sinaiticus in 1844 and 1859 in the monastery of St. Katharine on Mount Sinai. In the year last named I was traveling in the East under the patronage of Emperor Alexander II of Russia, and to him it was my good fortune to transfer the manuscript. It contains the Old and New Testaments and is written with four columns to a page. The New Testament is perfect, not having been deprived of a single leaf. To the twenty-seven books of the New Testament are appended the epistle of Barnabas complete and part of the Shepherd of Hermas, which books, even at the beginning of the fourth century, were reckoned for Holy Scripture by a good many. We are led, by all the data upon which we calculate the antiquity of manuscripts, to assign the Codex Sinaiticus to the middle of the fourth century. The evidence in favor of so great an age is more certain in the case of the Sinaitic Codex than in that of the Vatican manuscript. It is even not impossible that the Sinaitic Codex—we cannot say as much of the Vatican manuscript—formed one of the fifty copies of the Bible which in the year A.D. 331 the Emperor Constantine ordered to be executed for Constantinople under the direction of Eusebius, the Bishop of Cesarea, best known as a church historian. In this case it must be understood that the Emperor Justinina, the founder of the Sinaitic monastery, sent it as a present from Constantinople to the monks at Sinai. The manuscript was edited by the discoverer in 1862 at the cost of the Russian Emperor Alexander II, in a form as literally exact as it was splendid; the New Testament of the same was reproduced for ordinary use in a cheaper form in 1863 and 1865.

From all that has been said, it follows that the first place for antiquity and extent, among the three chief manuscripts, belongs to the Sinaitic Codex, the second place belongs to the Vatican, and the third to the Alexandrian. This arrangement is altogether confirmed by the condition of the text of the manuscripts. That text is not only in accordance with the writing of manuscripts in the fourth and fifth centuries, the same which was read in the East in precisely those centuries, but rather for the most part of it truly represents the text which was then copied from much earlier documents by Alexandrian scribes who knew very little of Greek and, therefore, did not intentionally make the least alteration—that is to say the very text which, in the second and third centuries, was spread over a great part of Christendom. In further confirmation of this idea we may refer to the agreement of our three ancient copies with the oldest translations, the Latin made in the second century in proconsular Africa, the Syriac version of the Gospels made at the same time and recently brought from the Nitrian desert in Egypt to the British Museum, and the Coptic or Egyptian versions of the third century. The same opinion is also further confirmed by the agreements of the text of the three great manuscripts with Irenaeus, Clement of Alexandria, Origen, and others of the older Fathers of the church. What we have been saying applies most of all to the Codex Sinaiticus, which, for example, is unapproachable in its close relation to the Latin version of the second century; it applies in a lesser degree to the Vatican manuscript, and still less to the Alexandrian, which, however, is far preferable in the Acts, Epistles, and Revelation to what it is in the Gospels.

There are two remarkable readings which are very instructive towards determining the age of the manuscripts and their authority, and these we shall forthwith take the liberty to lay before the reader.

1. The ordinary conclusion of the Gospel of Mark (16:9–21) is to be found in more than five hundred Greek manuscripts, in all Syriac end Coptic manuscripts, in almost all the Latin, and in the Gothic version. But Eusebius and Jerome say expressly that in nearly all correct copies of their time, Mark's gospel ended with the 8th verse of the last chapter and was without verses 9–21. With these famous accurate manuscripts of Eusebius (who died A.D. 340), there agree— among all extant Greek manuscripts—only the Sinaitic and the Vatican.

2. In the beginning of the epistle to the Ephesians we read, "to the saints which are at Epheaus;" but Marcion (A.D. 140), did not find the words "at Ephesus" in his copy. The same is true of Origen (A.D. 185–254); and Basil the Great (who died A.D. 379), affirmed that those words were wanting in old copies. And this omission accords very well with the encyclical or general character of the epistle. At the present day, our ancient Greek manuscripts, and all ancient versions, contain the words "at Ephesus;" yea, even Jerome knew no copy with a different reading. Now, only the Sinaitic and the Vatican correspond with the old copies of Basil and those of Orion and Marcion.

To these examples others might be added: thus Origen says on John 1:4, that in some copies it was written, "in Him is life," for "in Him was life." This is a reading which we find in sundry quotations

before the time of Origen; but only among all known Greek manuscripts it is only in the Sinaitic and the famous old Codex Beza, a
copy of the Gospels at Cambridge; yet it is also found in most of the
early Latin versions, in the most ancient Syriac, and in the oldest
Coptic. Again, in Matthew 13:35, Jerome observes that in the third
century Porphyry, the antagonist of Christianity, had found fault
with the evangelist Matthew for having said, "which was spoken by
the prophet Esaias." A writing of the second century had already
witnessed to the same reading, but Jerome adds further that well-
informed men had long ago removed the name of Esaias. Among all
our manuscripts of a thousand years old and upwards, there is not a
solitary example containing the name of Esaias in the text referred
to—except the Sinaitic, to which a few of less than a thousand years
old may be added. Once more Origen quotes John 13:10, six times;
but only the Sinaitic and several ancient Latin manuscripts read it
the same as Origen: "He that is washed needeth not to wash, but is
clean every whit." In John 6:5l, also, where the reading is very
difficult to settle, the Sinaitic is alone among all Greek copies indubi-
tably correct, and Tertullian, at the end of the second century, confirms the Sinaitic reading: "If any man eat of my bread, he shall live
for ever. The bread that I will give for the life of the world is my
flesh." We omit to indicate further illustrations of this kind, although there are many others like them.

While the text of the English Authorized Version is faithfully
represented in this work, such readings as differ from it in the three
great authorities are indicated in the notes. The letter S means the
Sinaitic manuscript, V the Vatican, and A the Alexandrian. S*, V*,
A* point out any reading of S, V, or A, which has been altered by
some later hand, although we give the original and not the altered
reading in such cases. When we give an altered reading, it is marked
S^2, V^2, or A^2; but as a rule only original readings are noted, and
reference is made seldom to changes introduced by ancient correc-
tors. The abbreviation "om" signifies the omission of the word or
words to which it refers; "adds" or "add," point to the omission of a
word or words in one or more of our manuscripts If two or more
notes belong to the same words of the text, they are divided by a

comma and not by a semicolon. If words of the text itself are quoted, they have after them the sign : , and then follow the readings of the Codices.

Sundry manifest slips of the pen which occur in the manuscripts, especially in those of the Alexandrian scribes, have been passed over in silence. Yet there are some which have been noted which are to be regarded as erroneous, even if not pointed out by the words "an error," or "a mere error." I have no doubt that in the very earliest ages after our Holy Scriptures were written and before the authority of the Church protected them, willful alterations and especially additions were made in them. Many various readings consist only in the forms of words and their arrangement and are of small import. Many others did not at all require to be noticed here because they merely relate to the Greek idiom. In some cases I have allowed myself to indicate an inaccurate or unsuitable rendering of the Greek, prefixing "translate," or "all MS." Distinguished scholars such as Trench, Scrivener, and Alford, whom I have usually followed in these cases, know how to supply still more of these rectications, but a larger introduction of them was not in accordance with the plan of this work.

For no single book of classic Greek antiquity is it possible to summon three primitive witnesses comparable to the Sinaitic, the Vatican, and the Alexandrian codices for the confirmation and rectification of its text. That we can manifestly do this in the case of the most holy and influential Book which the world possesses calls for our profoundest gratitude to the Lord our God.